MW01598320

TIMETABLES OF SPORTS HISTORY:
BASEBALL

BY
WILLIAM S. JARRETT

Facts On File
New York • Oxford

Baseball Timetables

Copyright © 1989 by William S. Jarrett

All rights reserved. No part of this book may be
reproduced or utilized in any form or by any
means, electronic or mechanical, including photo
copying, recording, or by any information storage
and retrieval systems, without permission in
writing from the publisher. For information
contact:

> Facts On File
> 460 Park Avenue South
> New York, New York 10016

British CIP data available on request
Interior Text Design by Ron Monteleone
Jacket Design by Ron Monteleone
Composition by Facts On File, Inc.
Printed in the United States of America
10 9 8 7 6 5 4 3 2 1

ISBN 0-8160-1918-5

All photographs are provided courtesy of the
National Baseball Library, Cooperstown, New York

This book is printed on acid-free paper.

796.357
JAR

CONTENTS

Preface   iv

How To Use This Book   v

Acknowledgments   vi

Major League Baseball 1903–1988   1

Index   87

PREFACE

Baseball Timetables tells the year-by-year story of America's favorite pastime in an entirely new and different way. Instead of listing row after row of statistics, this book brings to life, in words and pictures, the major events and the great performers that have made baseball what it is today.

Each page represents a year in the major leagues, beginning in 1903 when the first World Series was played between the Boston Red Sox and the Pittsburgh Pirates. The Red Sox won that Series behind the great pitching of Cy Young and Bill Dineen, beating the Pirates in 4 straight games after losing 3 out of the first 4 games. In the initial World Series, the winner had to take 5 games out of 9, instead of the current 4-out-of-7 format.

Of course, baseball bagan long before 1903. Anyone who has ever visited the Baseball Hall of Fame in Cooperstown, New York, knows that Abner Doubleday laid out the first baseball diamond there back in 1839. Some baseball experts believe that Alexander J. Cartwright of New York is the real "Father of Baseball," but the important thing to remember is that baseball was, and remains, a very special game.

When you think about it, baseball differs from other sports in many ways, making it the unique game that it is. It's the only sport, for example, in which the team that has the ball is on the defense, not the offense. The only way to score in baseball is for a runner to cross home plate *without the ball*. Unlike every other game that's played with a ball, the baseball itself does not do the scoring. And baseball is also the only game that is not governed in some way by the clock—you have to keep playing until someone wins, unless the lights go out or it starts to rain or snow, in which case the game is rescheduled.

The first "organized" game of baseball was played in 1846 at the Elysian Fields in Hoboken, New Jersey between the Knickerbocker Baseball Club of New York and a pick-up team that called itself, simply, the New York Club. Soon other teams (called clubs) began playing in the New York area, including the Gothams, Eagles, Empires and Mutuals. The game did not progress much, though, until the Civil War, when soldiers on both sides of the conflict took up baseball in earnest.

Following the Civil War, the first semi-professional teams began to travel around the country, with teams representing Cincinnati and Chicago leading the way. They were succeeded by others, until finally, in 1876, the National League of Professional Baseball Clubs was formed in New York. It included teams from Philadelphia, Boston, St. Louis, New York, Cincinnati, Hartford, Louisville and Chicago. The National League remained the only "major" league until 1901, when the American League was formed under the leadership of Charles Comiskey of Chicago, Connie Mack of Philadelphia and Ban Johnson, president of the failing Western League. By 1903, the two leagues had resolved their differences and the first World Series was played. The rest, as they say, is history—and that's what *Baseball Timetables* is all about.

HOW TO USE THIS BOOK

Each page of *Baseball Timetables*—representing a year of major league baseball—is divided into three columns. The first is Regular Season. It displays the pennant-winning teams from each league, provides their won-lost records and details the records and statistics of their top players. The second column is All-Star and Postseason Games. Here you'll find a brief description of each All-Star contest (which began in 1933), League Championship Series (which began in 1969) and World Series. Game highlights and important records are covered. Column three is Awards & Honors. This column lists all players inducted into baseball's Hall of Fame (beginning in 1936) and the American and National League winners of the three major awards: Most Valuable Player (1922), Rookie of the Year (1947) and Cy Young (1956). [Note: The first year players were inducted into the Hall of Fame was 1936; the MVP was first awarded in 1922; the Rookie of the Year Award began in 1947; and the Cy Young Award was first given in 1956.] Additionally, the star pitchers, hitters and base stealers from each league are indicated, along with their statistics.

ACKNOWLEDGMENTS

I wish to thank Pat Kelly and her colleagues at the National Baseball Hall of Fame and Museum for their help in acquiring the photographs that bring these pages to life. Also, thanks go to Terri Stramiello for her help in researching the thousands of facts and details that have gone into these pages.

1903

REGULAR SEASON

American League
Boston (91-47) finishes 14½ games in front of Philadelphia. Cy Young (28-9), Bill Dineen (21-13) and Long Tom Hughes (20-7) head up a strong mound corps (2.57 ERA). Buck Freeman (3 HRs, 104 RBI) and Patsy Dougherty (.331, 195 hits) lead the team in hitting.

National League
Pittsburgh (91-49) clinches the pennant 6½ games in front of New York. Honus Wagner (.335, 101 RBI) and Fred Clarke (.351) pace the hitters. Deacon Phillippe (24-7) and Sam Leever (25- 7, 2.06 ERA) lead the pitching staff, which accounts for 16 shutouts during the season.

Cy Young (shown here in a Cleveland uniform, c. 1911) wins 28 games for the Boston Red Sox en route to a career record of 511 victories.

WORLD SERIES

The first "official" World Series is played in Boston between the Red Sox (AL) and the Pittsburgh Pirates (NL). The 1903 Series, played on a "best 5-out-of-9" basis, is won in a mild upset by Boston, 5 games to 3. After losing 3 out of the first 4 games, the Red Sox rally to win 4 in a row behind the pitching of Cy Young (2-1) and Bill Dineen (3-1, including 2 shutouts).

AWARDS & HONORS

AL Pitching Leaders
Cy Young (Boston) leads all hurlers with 28 wins and 2 saves. Earl Moore (Cleveland) has a 1.77 ERA, best in the AL. Rube Waddell (Philadelphia) strikes out 302.

AL Batting & Base Running Leaders
Nap Lajoie (Cleveland) hits .355 to beat out Sam Crawford for the batting title. Buck Freeman (Boston) hits 13 home runs and drives in 104 runs to lead the league. Harry Bay (Cleveland) steals 45 bases.

NL Pitching Leaders
Joe "Iron Man" McGinnity (New York) wins 31 games (one more than teammate Christy Mathewson) and wins both ends of a double-header for the 3d time in his career. Sam Leever (Pittsburgh) has the best ERA (2.06), and Mathewson fans 267. Carl Lundgren (Chicago) and Roscoe Miller (New York) each have 3 saves. Chick Fraser of Philadelphia tosses a no-hitter against Chicago, 10-0.

NL Batting & Base Running Leaders
Honus Wagner (Pittsburgh) bats .355 to lead the league. Jimmy Sheckard (Brooklyn) is tops in home runs (9), and Sam Mertes (New York) drives home 104. Frank Chance (Chicago) and Sheckard tie for most stolen bases (67).

1904

REGULAR SEASON

American League
The Boston Red Sox (95-59) repeat as pennant winners by only 1½ games over New York. Boston's veteran pitching staff of Cy Young (26-16), Bill Dineen (23-14) and Jesse Tannehill (21-11) produces the league's best team ERA (2.12). Young pitches the first "perfect game" in the major leagues, retiring 27 men in a row (May 5). Buck Freeman leads the team in RBI (84) and home runs (7).

National League
The New York Giants (106-47), led by manager John McGraw, finish 13 games in front of their nearest rival (Chicago). Pitchers Joe "Iron Man" McGinnity (35-8, 1.61 ERA) and Christy Mathewson (33-12, 2.03 ERA) dominate the league. Bill Dahlen leads the team (and the league) in RBI (80).

New York Giants' manager **John McGraw** (center) poses with his two 30-game winning pitchers **Christy Mathewson** (l.) and **"Iron Man" Joe McGinnity.**

WORLD SERIES

[Note: No World Series is held in 1904. An argument between the American and National Leagues—prompted in part by the National League's loss in the first World Series (1903)—causes a suspension of the games. (Formed back in 1876, the National League was embarrassed to lose the Series to the new American League, formed in 1901.) After the season the two leagues come to an agreement and make plans to resume the games in 1905.]

AWARDS & HONORS

AL Pitching Leaders
Jack Chesbro (New York) wins 41 games (an all-time record) to lead AL pitchers. Addie Joss (Cleveland) compiles the best ERA (1.59), followed closely by Rube Waddell (Philadelphia), who is #1 in strikeouts (349). Washington's Casey Patten is credited with 3 saves. Cy Young pitches a perfect game and teammate Jesse Tannehill tosses a no-hitter.

AL Batting & Base Running Leaders
Nap Lajoie (Cleveland) leads the AL in batting for the 2d year in a row (.381) and also finishes on top with 102 RBI. Harry Davis (Philadelphia) smacks 10 HRs. Elmer Flick (Cleveland) is first in stolen bases (42).

NL Pitching Leaders
Joe "Iron Man" McGinnity (New York) produces the lowest ERA (1.61), posts the most wins (35) and saves (5). His Giant teammate, Christy Mathewson, fans 212.

NL Batting & Base Running Leaders
Honus Wagner (Pittsburgh) takes the NL batting title for the 2d year in a row (.349). He also leads in stolen bases (53). Bill Dahlen (New York) leads in RBI (80). Harry Lumley (Brooklyn) hits the most home runs (9).

1905

REGULAR SEASON

American League
Philadelphia Athletics (92-56), led by manager Connie Mack, edge out the Chicago White Sox by 2 games to win the pennant. Boston, which won in 1903 and 1904, sinks to 4th place. Eddie Plank (25-12), Rube Waddell (26-11) and Andy Coakley (20-7) lead the A's pitching staff with 20 shutouts and 895 strikeouts. First baseman Harry Davis leads the offense, which tops the league in runs scored (617) and slugging percentage (.339).

National League
New York Giants (105-48), under John McGraw, repeat as NL champions, beating out Pittsburgh by 9 games. Christy Mathewson (31-8), Joe McGinnity (21-15) and Red Ames (22-8) head up the Giant pitching staff, which accounts for 760 strikeouts during the season. Left fielder Sam Mertes leads the team with 108 RBI and right fielder Mike Donlin hits .356

Hall of Famer **Rube Waddell's** 2.16 lifetime ERA ranks 6th among major league pitchers.

WORLD SERIES

After a one-year absence, the World Series returns to baseball, with the New York Giants playing the Philadelphia Athletics. With the format a "best 4-out-of-7" for the first time, New York wins the Series 4 games to 1 giving up no earned runs. In fact, all five games are won by shutouts. (Philadelphia's only victory comes on unearned runs.) New York ace Christy Mathewson hurls 3 shutouts and Joe McGinnity adds another to silence Philadelphia's bats completely. In 3 games, Mathewson allows a total of no runs, 14 hits, and one walk. Chief Bender (Philadelphia) tosses a 4-hit shutout for the A's only win. Dan McGann, Giant first baseman, drives home all 4 runs in game 3.

AWARDS & HONORS

AL Pitching Leaders
Rube Waddell (Philadelphia) dominates the league with most wins (26), most strikeouts (287), lowest ERA (1.48) and most saves (4). Weldon Henley (Philadelphia), Frank Smith (Chicago) and Bill Dineen (Boston) all hurl no-hit, no-run games.

AL Batting & Base Running Leaders
Elmer Flick (Cleveland) edges out Willie Keeler (New York) for the batting crown (.306 to .302). Harry Davis (Philadelphia) has the most HRs (8), most RBI (83) and most doubles (47). Danny Hoffman (Philadelphia) leads in stolen bases (46).

NL Pitching Leaders
Christy Mathewson (New York) captures most of the honors with most wins (31), best ERA (1.27), and most strikeouts (206). He also hurls a no-hit, no-run game against Chicago. Claude Elliott (New York) registers 6 saves.

NL Batting & Base Running Leaders
Cy Seymour (Cincinnati) wins the batting title (.377). He also leads the league in RBI (121), hits (219), doubles (40) and triples (21). His teammate, Fred Odwell, hits a league-high 9 home runs. Art Devlin (New York) has the most stolen bases (59).

1906

REGULAR SEASON

American League

The Chicago White Sox (93-58) end the season on top by 3 games over New York and 5 over Cleveland. The pitching staff, led by Doc White (18-6), Frank Owen (22-13) and Nick Altrock (20-13) posts 32 shutouts during the season. George Davis leads the White Sox at bat with 80 RBI (but no HRs).

National League

The Chicago Cubs (116-36) romp home 20 full games ahead of their closest pursuer (New York), winning a record-shattering number of games. Mordecai "Three Finger" Brown sets the pace for Chicago's great pitching staff, winning 26 games (including 10 shutouts) with an amazing ERA of 1.04. Ed Reulbach (19-4) and Jack Pfiester (20-8) lead a staff in which 5 pitchers have ERAs under 2.00. Third baseman Harry Steinfeldt leads the club in hitting (.377, 83 RBI) and leads all third basemen in fielding (.954).

WORLD SERIES

The first (and only) all-Chicago World Series ends with the White Sox on top, 4 games to 2. The opening game is played in bitterly cold weather, with snowflakes falling on the Windy City. George Davis and Frank Isbell star on offense for the White Sox, with both men batting .308 and Davis driving in 6 runs. Sox hurler Ed Walsh wins 2 games and strikes out 17 Cub batters, including a record-breaking 12 strikeouts in game 3.

AWARDS & HONORS

AL Pitching Leaders

Al Orth (New York) has the most wins (27). Rube Waddell (Philadelphia) leads in strikeouts (196) for the 5th year in a row and ties Otto Hess (Cleveland) with 3 saves. Doc White (Chicago) produces the lowest ERA (1.52).

AL Batting & Base Running Leaders

George Stone (St. Louis) bats .358 to lead the league. Harry Davis (Philadelphia) is the RBI leader for the 2d straight year (96) and hits the most HRs (12). Elmer Flick (Cleveland) and John Anderson (Washington) tie for most stolen bases (39).

NL Pitching Leaders

"Three Finger" Brown has the lowest ERA (1.04) having pitched 10 shutouts. Joe "Iron Man" McGinnity (New York) picks up the most wins (27), and Fred Beebe leads in strikeouts (171). New York's George Ferguson's 6 saves lead the league. John Lush (Philadelphia) and Mal Eason (Brooklyn) each hurl no-hitters.

NL Batting & Base Running Leaders

Honus Wagner (Pittsburgh) leads the senior circuit in batting (.339). Harry Steinfeldt (Chicago) and Jim Nealon (Pittsburgh) have the most RBI (83). Tim Jordan (Brooklyn) blasts 12 HRs. Frank Chance (Chicago) steals the most bases (57) and scores the most runs (103).

The **Cubs** and **White Sox** face each other in the all-Chicago World Series of 1906. (The White Sox win the Series, 4 games to 2.)

1907

REGULAR SEASON

American League

Detroit (92-58), led by its new superstar, Ty Cobb, clinches the pennant by a narrow 1½-game margin over Philadelphia. Cobb leads the league in every important offensive department (see *Awards & Honors*) with teammate Sam Crawford close behind (.323, 81 RBI). The Tiger pitching staff is led by Ed Killian (25-13) and Wild Bill Donovan (25-4).

National League

The Chicago Cubs (107-45) win again by a landslide, finishing 17 games in front of Pittsburgh. The phrase, "Tinkers-to-Evers-to-Chance," referring to Chicago's great double-play combination, is by now a familiar one in the baseball world. The Cubs' potent pitching staff leads the way, starring "Three Finger" Brown (20-6), Ed Reulbach (17-4), Jack Pfiester (15-9), Carl Lundgren (18-7) and Orval Overall (23-8).

WORLD SERIES

The Chicago Cubs avenge their World Series defeat in 1906 by sweeping the hard-hitting Detroit Tigers, 4 games to 0. No home runs are hit in the Series for the 3d year in a row, as pitching continues to dominate the game. The opening game is tied at 3-3 in the 12th inning when the game is called on account of darkness, ruining Wild Bill Donovan's brilliant pitching performance (12 strikeouts) for the Tigers. Superstar Ty Cobb has only 4 hits in the Series. "Three Finger" Brown completes the 4-game sweep for the Cubs, pitching the first and only shutout of the Series. Chicago's Jimmy Slagle, Johnny Evers and Frank Chance lead the fast Cubs on the bases with 18 stolen bases.

AWARDS & HONORS

AL Pitching Leaders

Big Ed Walsh (Chicago) turns in the lowest ERA (1.60) and ties 2 other pitchers with 4 saves. Chicago's Doc White has most wins (27, tied with Addie Joss of Cleveland). Rube Waddell (Philadelphia) strikes out 232, the 6th year in a row he has led in that department.

AL Batting & Base Running Leaders

Ty Cobb dominates the major leagues with an amazing record: .350 batting average; 212 hits; 49 stolen bases and 116 RBI. Harry Davis (Philadelphia) manages to keep Cobb from winning the Triple Crown by out-homering him 8 to 5.

NL Pitching Leaders

Christy Mathewson (New York) earns the most wins (24) and strikeouts (178). Jack Pfiester (Chicago) has the best ERA (1.15). Joe "Iron Man" McGinnity gets 4 saves. Frank Pfeffer (Boston) and Nick Maddox (Pittsburgh) both toss no-hitters.

NL Batting & Base Running Leaders

Honus Wagner (Pittsburgh) leads the league in hitting for the 4th time in 5 years (.350). He also steals the most bases (61) and raps out the most doubles (38). Sherry Magee (Philadelphia) leads in RBI (85) to edge out Ed Abbaticchio (Pittsburgh). Dave Brain (Boston) slams 10 HRs.

Honus Wagner, the **"Flying Dutchman,"** has a lifetime batting average of .329 and collects 3,430 hits. In 1936 Wagner is among the first players inducted into baseball's Hall of Fame.

1908

REGULAR SEASON

American League

Detroit (90-63) repeats as the pennant winner, but only by the narrowest margin of ½ game over Cleveland and 1½ games ahead of Chicago. Ed Summers (24-12) makes his pitching debut in the big leagues a successful one. He and veteran Wild Bill Donovan (18-7) lead a good Tiger pitching staff. Outfielder Ty Cobb continues his role as a one-man offense (see *Awards & Honors*), with help from Sam Crawford (.311, 80 RBI).

National League

The Chicago Cubs (99-55) win their 2d pennant in a row, but only by a game over New York and Pittsburgh in a torrid 3-team race that goes down to the wire. Cub pitchers "Three Finger" Brown (29-9) and Ed Reulbach (24-7) lead the way. The weak Cub offense (.249 team average) is offset by the best defense in the major leagues (206 errors and .969 fielding average).

WORLD SERIES

The Chicago Cubs repeat as World Series champions, defeating Detroit again, 4 games to 1, including consecutive shutouts in the final 2 games. In the opening game, Chicago scores 5 runs in the 9th inning to snatch victory from the Tigers on a rain-drenched field. Joe Tinker, Cub shortstop, hits the only home run in the last four World Series. Pitcher Orval Overall picks up 2 wins for the Cubs, including the Series clincher. Ty Cobb, frustrated in World Series play so far, erupts with 4 hits in game 3, Detroit's first World Series win ever.

Ed Walsh (shown here with the 1917 Boston Braves) wins 40 games for the Chicago White Sox, including 11 shutouts. His career ERA of 1.82 still ranks #1 among all major league pitchers.

AWARDS & HONORS

AL Pitching Leaders

Addie Joss (Cleveland) has the league's best ERA (1.16) and pitches a perfect game. Ed Walsh (Chicago) notches the most strikeouts (269) and has the most wins (40, including 11 shutouts) and saves (6). Cy Young (Boston), Bob Rhodes (Cleveland) and Frank Smith (Chicago) all toss no-hitters during the season.

AL Batting & Base Running Leaders

Ty Cobb (Detroit) repeats as batting champion (.324). He also has most RBI (108), most doubles (36), most triples (20), and the highest slugging average (.475). Teammate Sam Crawford leads in HRs with 7, and Patsy Dougherty (Chicago) steals the most bases (47).

NL Pitching Leaders

Christy Mathewson (New York) posts the most wins (37) and saves (5, tied with "Three Finger" Brown) and fans a total of 259. His ERA (1.43) also leads the league. George Wiltse (New York) and Nap Rucker (Brooklyn) record no-hit games during the season.

NL Batting & Base Running Leaders

Honus Wagner (Pittsburgh) again leads the NL hit parade with the highest average (.354), most RBI (109), hits (201), doubles (39) and triples (19). He also leads with 53 stolen bases. Tim Jordan (Brooklyn) clouts 12 HRs.

1909

REGULAR SEASON

American League
The Detroit Tigers (98-54) capture their 3d straight pennant, beating out the Philadelphia A's by 3½ games. Ed Summers (19- 9), George Mullin (29-8) and Ed Willett (21-10) provide strong pitching, while the unstoppable Ty Cobb continues to tear the league apart with his bat and base running.

National League
Pittsburgh (110-42) grabs the pennant away from the Chicago Cubs (104-49), providing the great Honus Wagner with a chance to play in another World Series. Like his AL counterpart, Ty Cobb, Wagner tops the league in most batting categories (see *Awards & Honors*). The Pirate pitching staff features Howie Camnitz (25-6), Vic Willis (22-11) and Lefty Leifield (19-8). Coupled with a strong defense, the team is solid all around.

WORLD SERIES

Detroit fails to win in its 3d straight World Series, losing this time to Pittsburgh, 4 games to 3. It is the first time the Series has gone the full 7 games. The closely matched teams alternate victories for the first 6 games. Then, in the 7th and deciding game, Pittsburgh's Babe Adams (12-3 during the regular season) wins his 3d game of the Series with a 6-hit shutout. Honus Wagner outshines Detroit's Ty Cobb in the Series with 6 steals, 8 hits, and 6 RBI (vs. Cobb's 2 steals, 6 hits and 6 RBI).

AWARDS & HONORS

AL Pitching Leaders
George Mullin's 29 wins for Detroit are tops in the AL. Harry Krause (Philadelphia) leads in ERA with 1.39, and Frank Smith (Chicago) has the most strikeouts (177). Frank Arellanes (Boston) has a league-leading 8 saves.

AL Batting & Base Running Leaders
Ty Cobb (Detroit) wins the Triple Crown with the highest batting average (.377), most home runs (9) and most RBI (107). He also steals 76 bases to lead the league.

NL Pitching Leaders
Christy Mathewson (25-6), now in his 10th year with New York, continues his amazing career with the best ERA (1.14). "Three Finger" Brown (Chicago) records the most wins (27) and most saves (7), while Orval Overall (Chicago) fans 205. Leon Ames (New York) pitches the year's only no-hit game (for 9 innings) but loses the game and no-hitter in the 13th.

NL Batting & Base Running Leaders
Honus Wagner (Pittsburgh) again leads the league in most categories, including batting average (.339) and RBI (100). Red Murray (New York) smacks the most HRs (7), and Bob Bescher (Cincinnati) steals the most bases (54).

1910

REGULAR SEASON

American League
Philadelphia (102-48) takes the pennant with ease, ending the season 14½ games in front of New York. Jack Coombs (31-9) is the new ace of Connie Mack's pitching staff, along with veteran hurler Chief Bender (23-5). Eddie Collins (.322, 81 RBI) and rookie Frank Baker (.283, 74 RBI) top the offense, which leads the league in team batting (.266).

National League
The Chicago Cubs (104-50) win their 4th pennant in 5 years with "Three Finger" Brown (25-13) and King Cole (20-4) in control of the pitching staff. "Wildfire" Schulte (.301, 10 HRs, 68 RBI) and Solly Hofman (.325, 86 RBI) supply the power. Chicago's defense, featuring the famous "Tinkers-to-Evers-to-Chance" infield, is again superior, committing only 230 errors during the season.

WORLD SERIES

Backed by the great pitching of Jack Coombs and the hitting of Danny Murphy (.350, 8 RBI) and Frank Baker (.409), the Philadelphia A's take the 1910 World Series from the Cubs, 4 games to 1. In the opening game, Frank Baker gets 3 hits and 2 RBI to back up Chief Bender's 3-hitter. The Cubs avoid a sweep by tying game 4 in the 9th on Frank Chance's triple and then winning it in the 10th. Coombs picks up his 3d win of the Series in the final game. The usually reliable Cub defense makes 12 errors in the 5-game Series.

AWARDS & HONORS

AL Pitching Leaders
Ed Walsh (Chicago) leads all AL pitchers with an ERA of 1.27. He also ties Charley Hall (Boston) with 5 saves. Jack Coombs (Philadelphia) has the most wins (31), and Walter Johnson (Washington) strikes out 313 in his first big year. Chief Bender (Philadelphia), Addie Joss (Cleveland) and Tom Hughes (New York) turn in no-hitters, but Hughes loses game (and no-hitter) in extra innings.

AL Batting & Base Running Leaders
Ty Cobb (Detroit) is AL batting champion for 4th year in a row (.385). He also leads in runs scored (106). Teammate Sam Crawford drives in 120 runs and Eddie Collins (Philadelphia) takes over Cobb's base-stealing crown with 81 thefts. Jake Stahl (Boston) clouts 10 HRs.

NL Pitching Leaders
Christy Mathewson (New York) has the most wins (27) and George McQuillan (Philadelphia) allows the fewest earned runs (1.60) per game, while his teammate Earl "Crossfire" Moore strikes out 185. "Three Finger" Brown saves 7 games for Chicago.

NL Batting & Base Running Leaders
Sherry Magee (Philadelphia) has a big year, leading the league in batting (.331), RBI (123) and runs scored (110). "Wildfire" Schulte (Chicago) and Fred Beck (Boston) each slug a league-leading 10 HRs.

REGULAR SEASON

American League
Connie Mack's Philadelphia Athletics (101-50) win their second straight pennant, finishing far ahead (13½ games) of 2d-place Detroit. The pitching of Jack Coombs (28-12), Eddie Plank (23-8) and Chief Bender (17-5) is superior. Frank Baker (.334, 115 RBI) leads the offense, which boasts the best batting (.296) and slugging (.397) averages in the AL.

National League
The New York Giants (99-54) win their 2d pennant under John McGraw, beating out their closest rival (Chicago) by 7½ games. Veteran ace Christy Mathewson (26-13, 1.99 ERA) heads the pitching staff along with young Rube Marquard (24-7). Larry Doyle (.310, 13 HRs, 77 RBI) and Fred Merkle (.283, 12 HRs, 84 RBI) are offensive standouts.

WORLD SERIES

The Philadelphia Athletics, behind the pitching of Jack Coombs, Chief Bender and Eddie Plank, are too much for Christy Mathewson and his New York Giants. The A's win the Series, 4 games to 2. Bender wins 2 games and strikes out 20, while Coombs (1-0) fans 16 in 20 innings. Frank Baker (.375) smacks 2 HRs, scores 7 times, and has 5 RBI to lead the offense. Larry Doyle and Chief Meyers are the only Giants to get more than 5 hits in the Series.

AWARDS & HONORS

Most Valuable Players
AL: Ty Cobb (Detroit)
NL: Frank "Wildfire" Schulte (Chicago)

AL Pitching Leaders
Jack Coombs (Philadelphia) picks up the most wins (28), while teammate Eddie Plank achieves 5 saves. Vean Gregg (Cleveland), a rookie, has the lowest ERA (1.81), and Ed Walsh (Chicago) has the most strikeouts (255). Walsh and Smoky Joe Wood (Boston) both toss no-hitters.

AL Batting & Base Running Leaders
Ty Cobb (Detroit) is the batting champion for the 5th consecutive year with a record-breaking .420 average. He also drives in 144 runs, has 248 hits (including 47 doubles and 24 triples), scores 147 runs and steals 83 bases (a new major league record). Frank "Homerun" Baker earns his nickname, hitting a league-high 11 HRs.

NL Pitching Leaders
Rookie pitcher Grover Cleveland Alexander (Philadelphia) amazes the baseball world, winning 28 games to lead the league. Christy Mathewson (New York) records the best ERA (1.99), and teammate Rube Marquard fans 237. "Three Finger" Brown (Chicago) chalks up 13 saves.

NL Batting & Base Running Leaders
Honus Wagner (Pittsburgh) wins the batting championship (.334) for the 7th time, beating out Doc Miller (Boston) by one percentage point. Miller has the most hits (192). Frank "Wildfire" Schulte (Chicago) smacks 21 homers and drives in 121 runs to lead the league in both categories. Bob Bescher (Cincinnati) steals 81 bases, a new NL record.

Ty Cobb slides safely into third under **Frank "Homerun" Baker's** tag. Cobb enjoyed his greatest season in 1911, with career–high totals in hits (248), doubles (47), triples (24), runs (147), RBI (144) and batting average (.420).

1912

REGULAR SEASON

American League
The Boston Red Sox (105-47) go from last place to first in one year to grab the pennant by 14 games over Washington. Smoky Joe Wood (34-5), Buck O'Brien (20-13) and Hugh Bedient (20-9) are all surprise 20-game winners. Boston's pitching staff produces a league-leading 18 shutouts and 108 complete games. Tris Speaker (.383, 10 HRs, 98 RBI) and Duffy Lewis (.284, 109 RBI) supply the power as Red Sox score 799 runs while holding their opponents to 544.

National League
New York (103-48) retains the NL championship, finishing ahead of Pittsburgh by 10 games. The Giants' mound trio of Christy Mathewson (23-12), Rube Marquard (26-11) and Jeff Tesreau (17-7) leads a pitching staff whose ERA (2.58) is lowest in the NL. Larry Doyle (.330, 10 HRs, 90 RBI) and Fred Merkle (.309, 11 HRs, 84 RBI) again pace the Giant attack.

WORLD SERIES

In an exciting 7-game Series, the Boston Red Sox come out on top over the New York Giants, as Smoky Joe Wood wins 3 games and strikes out 21. The final game goes into extra innings, with Christy Mathewson, the Giant ace, dueling Hugh Bedient and Smoky Joe Wood (in relief). The winning run scores in the 10th on a sacrifice fly. Tris Speaker (.300), Harry Hooper (.290) and Jake Stahl (.281) collect 9 hits each and score 10 runs to lead Boston's offense. Buck Herzog bats .400 to lead the Giants. Despite allowing only 5 earned runs over 28⅔ innings, Mathewson has an 0-2 record for the Series.

AWARDS & HONORS

Most Valuable Players
AL: Tris Speaker (Boston)
NL: Larry Doyle (New York)

AL Pitching Leaders
Smoky Joe Wood (Boston) leads all pitchers with 34 wins (including 10 shutouts). Walter Johnson (Washington) compiles the lowest ERA (1.39) and most strikeouts (303). Ed Walsh (Chicago) leads the AL with 10 saves. George Mullin (Detroit) and Earl Hamilton (St. Louis) toss no-hitters.

AL Batting & Base Running Leaders
Ty Cobb (Detroit) finishes over .400 for the 2d year in a row (.410) and collects the most hits (227). Frank Baker (Philadelphia) leads in RBI (133) and ties Tris Speaker (Boston) for most HRs (10). Clyde Milan (Washington) breaks Cobb's stolen-base record (set in 1911) with 88 thefts.

NL Pitching Leaders
Jeff Tesreau (New York) has the lowest ERA (1.96) and tosses a no-hitter (the only one in NL). Teammate Rube Marquard ties Larry Cheney (Chicago) for most wins (26). Grover Cleveland Alexander (Philadelphia) strikes out 195. Slim Sallee has 6 saves.

NL Batting & Base Running Leaders
Heinie Zimmerman (Chicago) wins the Triple Crown with highest batting average (.372), most RBI (103), most hits (207) and most HRs (14). Bob Bescher (Cincinnati) leads in stolen bases (67).

1913

REGULAR SEASON

American League

Connie Mack's Philadelphia Athletics (96-57) win for the 3d time in 4 years, finishing 6½ games in front of the Washington Senators. The A's fine pitching staff is led by Eddie Plank (18-10), Chief Bender (21-10) and "Boardwalk" Brown (17-7). Frank "Homerun" Baker's hitting (.336, 12 HRs, 126 RBI) keys the A's attack, aided by Eddie Collins (.345) and Stuffy McInnis (.326, 90 RBI).

National League

John McGraw's New York Giants (101-51) repeat as NL champions, leading Philadelphia by 12½ games. Christy Mathewson (25-11), Rube Marquard (23-10) and Jeff Tesreau (22-13) head up a pitching staff with an ERA of 2.43. Chief Meyers (.312) is the only regular to bat over .300 (and yet team batting average of .273 leads the NL).

During his 21–year career with the Washington Senators, **Walter "Big Train" Johnson** leads the American League in strikeouts 12 times and wins 416 games (2d best in major league history).

WORLD SERIES

The Philadelphia Athletics win their 3d world championship in a row, beating New York 4 games to 1. Superior pitching once again makes the difference, as Chief Bender (2-0), Smoky Joe Bush (who pitches a 5-hit shutout in his only appearance) and Eddie Plank (2 earned runs in 19 innings) excel. In a losing cause, Giant pitching ace Christy Mathewson also allows only 2 earned runs in 19 innings of work. Frank Baker (9 hits, 7 RBI and .450 average) and Eddie Collins (.421) are the batting heroes for Philadelphia. Larry McLean (.500) paces the New York attack.

AWARDS & HONORS

Most Valuable Players

AL: Walter Johnson (Washington)
NL: Jake Daubert (Brooklyn)

AL Pitching Leaders

Walter Johnson (Washington) leads all pitchers with 36 wins and 243 strikeouts. He also sets a new record by pitching 56 consecutive innings without allowing a run. His ERA (1.09) is the lowest ever. Chief Bender (Philadelphia) has the most saves (12).

AL Batting & Base Running Leaders

Ty Cobb (Detroit) takes his 7th straight batting title (.390). Frank Baker (Philadelphia) is the RBI leader (126) and home-run champ (12). Clyde Milan (Washington) steals 75 bases.

NL Pitching Leaders

Tom Seaton (Philadelphia) has the most wins (27) and strikeouts (168), but Christy Mathewson (New York) produces the lowest ERA (2.06). Larry Cheney (Chicago) earns the most saves (11).

NL Batting & Base Running Leaders

Jake Daubert (Brooklyn) leads the league in batting (.350). Gavvy Cravath (Philadelphia) hits the most HRs (19), drives in the most runs (128) and bangs out the most hits (179). Max Carey (Pittsburgh) leads in stolen bases with 61.

1914

REGULAR SEASON

American League
The Philadelphia A's (99-53) continue to dominate the league, winning their 4th pennant in 5 years and finishing 8½ games ahead of Boston. Rookie pitchers Bob Shawkey (16-8) and Herb Pennock (11-4) join veterans Chief Bender (17-3), Joe Bush (16-12) and Eddie Plank (15-7) on a top-notch staff. Eddie Collins (.344, 85 RBI), Stuffy McInnis (.314, 95 RBI) and Frank Baker (.319, 97 RBI) are the leading hitters.

National League
The lowly Boston Braves (94-59), perennial cellar-dwellers, surprise the baseball world by finishing 10½ games ahead of New York. Bill James (26-7) and Dick Rudolph (27-10) star on the mound. Only one regular, Joe Connolly (.306), bats over .300. The defense produces 143 double plays, featuring Johnny Evers, second base, and Rabbit Maranville, shortstop.

Charles "Chief" Bender, the pitching ace for Connie Mack's pennant–winning Philadelphia Athletics.

WORLD SERIES

The surprising Boston Braves complete their dream season, beating the mighty Philadelphia Athletics in 4 straight games. Boston pitchers Dick Rudolph and Bill James each win 2 games, giving up only one earned run between them over 29 innings. Boston catcher Hank Gowdy hits the only HR in the series, bats .545 and has 5 extra base hits. Teammate Johnny Evers goes 6 for 17 (.438).

AWARDS & HONORS

Most Valuable Players
AL: Eddie Collins (Philadelphia)
NL: Johnny Evers (Boston)

AL Pitching Leaders
Walter Johnson (Washington) ends the season with the most wins (28) and most strikeouts (225). Dutch Leonard (Boston) posts a record low ERA (1.01). Six pitchers are tied with 4 saves. Joe Benz (Chicago) hurls a no-hitter. His teammate Jim Scott has a no-hitter through 9 innings, but loses it and the game in the 10th.

AL Batting & Base Running Leaders
Ty Cobb (Detroit) leads all AL hitters for the 8th year in a row (.368). Teammate Sam Crawford has the most RBI (104). Frank Baker (Philadelphia) leads in HRs (9) and Fritz Maisel (New York) steals the most bases (74).

NL Pitching Leaders
Bill Doak's (St. Louis) 1.72 ERA and Dick Rudolph's (Boston) 27 wins pace the league. Grover Cleveland Alexander (Philadelphia) strikes out 214. Cincinnati's Red Ames ties Slim Sallee (St. Louis) with 6 saves. George Davis (Boston) pitches the year's only no-hitter.

NL Batting & Base Running Leaders
Jake Daubert (Brooklyn) compiles a .329 batting average to lead the league. Sherry Magee (Philadelphia) is first with 103 RBI and teammate Gavvy Cravath hits the most homers (19). George Burns (New York) is the top base stealer (62).

REGULAR SEASON

American League

Boston's Red Sox (101-50) sneak in ahead of Detroit by 2½ games to win the AL pennant behind the steady pitching of Rube Foster (19-8), Smoky Joe Wood (15-5), Ernie Shore (19-8) and a rookie named Babe Ruth (18-8). Tris Speaker (.322) is the only regular to bat over .300.

National League

The Philadelphia Phillies (90-62) win their 1st pennant, beating out the defending champion Boston Braves by 7 games. Grover Cleveland Alexander (31-10) and Erskine Mayer (21-15) head the pitching corps (.217 team ERA). Fred Luderus (.315) and Gavvy Cravath (.285, 24 HR, 115 RBI) lead the offense.

Grover Cleveland Alexander leads the Phillies to the 1915 World Series with a 31–10 record (1.22 ERA). Alexander's 373 wins are 3d most in the majors and his 90 shutouts rank 2d.

WORLD SERIES

After losing the first game of the 1915 Series, the Boston Red Sox take the next 4 contests, beating the Philadelphia Phillies 4 games to 1. Rube Foster is Boston's pitching star with 2 wins and a 2.00 ERA. Duffy Lewis (.444) bangs out 8 hits and drives home 5 runs to lead the Sox. Teammate Harry Hooper smashes 2 homers in the final game. Fred Luderus (.438, 6 RBI) is the only Philadelphia regular to hit over .300.

AWARDS & HONORS

AL Pitching Leaders

Smoky Joe Wood (Boston) leads the league with 1.49 ERA. Walter Johnson (Washington) has the most wins (28) and most strikeouts (203). Carl Mays (Boston) earns 5 saves.

AL Batting & Base Running Leaders

Braggo Roth (Chicago/Cleveland) leads the league in home runs (7). Ty Cobb (Detroit) captures the batting crown for the 9th straight year (.369). Detroit teammates Sam Crawford and Bobby Veach tie for most RBI (112). Cobb, in his 11th year, steals 96 bases for a new major league record.

NL Pitching Leaders

Grover Cleveland Alexander's (Philadelphia) 31 wins (including 12 shutouts), 241 strikeouts and 1.22 ERA all lead the league. Boston's Tom Hughes ties Rube Benton (Cincinnati/New York) with 5 saves. Rube Marquard (New York) and Jimmy Lavender (Chicago) both turn in no-hitters.

NL Batting & Base Running Leaders

Larry Doyle (New York) leads NL in batting (.320). Gavvy Cravath (Boston) takes the honors for the most home runs (24) and most RBI (115). Max Carey (Pittsburgh) leads in stolen bases (36).

REGULAR SEASON

American League
Boston's Red Sox (91-63) repeat as AL champions, squeezing past Chicago and Detroit in the final week. Babe Ruth becomes a star pitcher (23-12, including 9 shutouts), backed up by Dutch Leonard (18-12), Ernie Shore (16-10) and Carl Mays (18-13). Boston's weak offense is balanced by a good defense, which commits the fewest errors (183) in the majors.

National League
The Brooklyn Dodgers (94-60) win their first pennant, beating out Philadelphia by 2½ games. Jeff Pfeffer (25-11) and Larry Cheney (18-12) each compiles a 1.92 ERA to head up a solid pitching staff (2.12 ERA). Zack Wheat (9 HRs, 73 RBI) is the top run producer. The New York Giants win 26 consecutive games during the 1916 season to set a major-league record.

WORLD SERIES

The Boston Red Sox repeat as world champions, winning 4 games to 1 over the Brooklyn Dodgers. Boston third baseman Larry Gardner accounts for 6 RBI with only 3 hits (2 are home runs). Babe Ruth makes his first start in a World Series game and hurls a 6-hitter over 14 innings to win game 2. Ernie Shore wins 2 games for Boston, including a 3-hitter in game 5, the clincher.

AWARDS & HONORS

AL Pitching Leaders
Babe Ruth (Boston) turns in the lowest ERA (1.75). Walter Johnson (Washington) picks up the most wins (25) and most strikeouts (228). Bob Shawkey (New York) is credited with 8 saves. George Foster (Boston), Joe Bush (Philadelphia) and Hub Leonard (Boston) all toss no-hitters in 1916.

AL Batting & Base Running Leaders
Tris Speaker (now with Cleveland) is the first batter to outhit Ty Cobb in 10 years (.386 to .371). Del Pratt (St. Louis) leads AL in RBI (103), and Cobb steals 68 bases. Wally Pipp (New York) cranks out 12 home runs.

NL Pitching Leaders
Grover Cleveland Alexander (Philadelphia) continues his great career with 33 wins (including a league-record 16 shutouts), lowest ERA (1.55) and most strikeouts (167). Red Ames (St. Louis) earns 7 saves. Tom Hughes (Boston) throws the NL's only no-hitter for 1916.

NL Batting & Base Running Leaders
Hal Chase (Cincinnati) wins the NL batting title (.339) and collects the most hits (184). Heinie Zimmerman (Chicago/New York) knocks in the most runs (83), and Max Carey (Pittsburgh) steals the most bases (63).

1917

REGULAR SEASON

American League
The Chicago White Sox (100-54) come on strong to win the pennant by 9 games over defending champion Boston. Ed Cicotte (28-12) heads the pitching staff, which posts the most shutouts (22) and best ERA (2.16) in the league. Happy Felsch (.308, 102 RBI) supplies the power and Eddie Collins, with 53 steals, leads the fastest team in the majors (219 stolen bases).

National League
John McGraw leads the New York Giants (98-56) to another pennant, beating the nearest rival (Philadelphia) by 10 games. Ferdie Schupp (21-7), Slim Sallee (18-7) and Pol Perritt (17-7) provide solid pitching. Heinie Zimmerman (.297, 102 RBI) and Dave Robertson (12 HRs) supply the batting punch. New York's defense commits only 208 errors and has the best fielding average (.968) in the NL.

WORLD SERIES

The Chicago White Sox capture their 2d World Series, defeating the New York Giants 4 games to 2. Red Faber is the pitching hero for Chicago, winning 3 games (2 in relief), including the game 6 clincher. Eddie Collins (.409) raps out 9 hits and steals 3 bases to lead the Chicago offense. Benny Kauff wallops 2 homers for New York in game 4 as Ferdie Schupp hurls New York's 2d shutout in a row.

AWARDS & HONORS

AL Pitching Leaders
Ed Cicotte's (Chicago) 1.53 ERA and 28 wins pace the league. Walter Johnson (Washington) is the strikeout king (188). Dave Danforth (Chicago) earns 9 saves. Ernie Shore (Boston) pitches a perfect game and 4 other AL pitchers produce no-hitters during 1917.

AL Batting & Base Running Leaders
After losing his batting title to Tris Speaker in 1916, Ty Cobb (Detroit) regains it with a .383 average on 223 hits (including 46 doubles and 23 triples). He also leads the league in stolen bases (55). Bobby Veach (Detroit) leads in RBI (103). Wally Pipp (New York) clouts 9 home runs.

NL Pitching Leaders
Grover Cleveland Alexander (now with Philadelphia) picks up the most wins (30) and leads in strikeouts (201). His ERA (1.86) is also best in the NL. In the first half of a doubleheader (May 2) Jim Vaughn (Chicago) hurls a no-hitter for 9 innings, then loses the game and no-hitter in the 10th. Fred Toney (Cincinnati) then pitches another no-hitter for 9 innings in the 2d game and wins it in the 10th after giving up a hit.

NL Batting & Base Running Leaders
Edd Roush (Cincinnati) is the league's leading hitter (.341). Heinie Zimmerman (New York) produces the most RBI (102). Gavvy Cravath (Philadelphia) and Dave Robertson (New York) tie for most HRs (12). Max Carey (Pittsburgh) is the top base stealer (46).

1918

REGULAR SEASON

American League

The Boston Red Sox (75-51) recapture the AL pennant they lost in 1917, winning by 2½ games over Cleveland (season is shortened to 128 games because of World War I). Babe Ruth's combined record as a pitcher (13-7, 2.22 ERA) and hitter (.300, 66 RBI) is unprecedented in professional baseball. Carl Mays (21-13) and Sad Sam Jones (16-5) also lead a staff that produces 26 shutouts and 105 complete games, best in the majors.

National League

The Chicago Cubs (84-45) win the pennant by 10½ games over New York with good defense and solid pitching. Hippo Vaughn (22-10), Claude Hendrix (19-7) and Lefty Tyler (19-9) combine for 19 shutouts. Charlie Hollocher (.316) is the only regular to bat over .300 for the season.

WORLD SERIES

The Boston Red Sox beat Chicago, 4 games to 2, to win their 3d world championship in 4 years. Babe Ruth (1.06 ERA) and Carl Mays (1.00 ERA) each win two games. Ruth's scoreless winning streak in World Series play ends at 29⅔ innings (game 4). Chicago's mound stars Hippo Vaughn and Lefty Tyler give up only 6 earned runs in 50 innings but receive poor offensive support. The Boston defense commits only one error in 6 games.

AWARDS & HONORS

AL Pitching Leaders

Walter Johnson's (Washington) 1.27 ERA leads all AL pitchers by a wide margin. He also has the most wins (23) and most strikeouts (162). New York's George Mogridge notches 7 saves. Hub Leonard (Boston) tosses his 2d career no-hitter.

AL Batting & Base Running Leaders

Ty Cobb (Detroit) wins the AL batting crown for the 11th time (.382). Babe Ruth (Boston) and Tilly Walker (Philadelphia) tie for most homers (11). Bobby Veach (Detroit) has the most RBI (78). George Sisler (St. Louis) is the stolen-base leader (45).

NL Pitching Leaders

Hippo Vaughn's (Chicago) 22 wins and 1.74 ERA and 148 strikeouts are tops in the league. Four pitchers earn 3 saves.

NL Batting & Base Running Leaders

Zack Wheat (Brooklyn) captures the NL batting title (.335) and Sherry Magee (Cincinnati) leads with 76 RBI. Gavvy Cravath (Philadelphia) wins home-run honors (8), and Pittsburgh's Max Carey steals the most bases (58) for the 5th time in 6 years.

1919

REGULAR SEASON

American League

The Chicago White Sox (88-52) regain the pennant they lost in 1918, edging out Cleveland by 3½ games (season is shortened again to 140 games because of World War I). Ed Cicotte (29-7) and Lefty Williams (23-11) star on the mound. Happy Felsch (86 RBI), Joe Jackson (.351, 96 RBI) and Eddie Collins (.319, 80 RBI) provide the offensive punch. Chicago's team batting average (.287) is best in the major leagues.

National League

The Cincinnati Reds (96-44) win their first pennant with good fielding and steady pitching (23 shutouts during the season). Slim Sallee (21-7), Dutch Ruether (19-6) and Hod Eller (20-9) are the mound mainstays. Edd Roush (.321, 71 RBI) and Heinie Groh (.310, 63 RBI) lead a team of average hitters. The Reds commit the fewest errors (152) in the league.

WORLD SERIES

Cincinnati continues to amaze the baseball world, beating Chicago in a new "5-out-of-9" Series format, 5 games to 3. [Note: It was later revealed that several White Sox players "fixed" the 1919 Series, in what has become known as the "Black Sox Scandal."] Hod Eller wins 2 games for the Reds, allowing only 2 earned runs per game. Lefty Williams of the White Sox loses 3 games (one in relief). Edd Roush and Greasy Neale lead the Cincinnati offense with 15 RBI.

AWARDS & HONORS

AL Pitching Leaders

Ed Cicotte (Chicago) registers the most wins (29). Walter Johnson (Washington) strikes out 147 and leads the league with 1.45 ERA. Allan Russell (New York/Boston) leads with 5 saves. Ray Caldwell (Boston) pitches a no-hitter.

AL Batting & Base Running Leaders

Ty Cobb's (Detroit) .384 average tops the league for the 12th time. He also ties teammate Bobby Veach for most hits (191). Babe Ruth (Boston), now playing in the outfield as well as pitching, leads the league in RBI (114) and home runs (29). Eddie Collins (Chicago) beats out Cobb for the stolen-base title (33).

NL Pitching Leaders

Grover Cleveland Alexander (Chicago) returns from a 1918 injury to lead the league in ERA (1.72). Hippo Vaughn (Chicago) has the most strikeouts (141) and Jesse Barnes (New York) picks up the most wins (25). Oscar Tuero is credited with 4 saves. Hod Eller (Cincinnati) twirls the only no-hitter of 1919.

NL Batting & Base Running Leaders

Edd Roush (Cincinnati) beats out Rogers Hornsby (St. Louis) for the batting crown (.321 to .318). Hy Meyers (Brooklyn) has the most RBI (73). George Burns (New York) swipes 40 bases.

1920

REGULAR SEASON

American League
The Cleveland Indians (98-56) capture the AL flag, nosing out Chicago by 2 games. Jim Bagby (31-12), Ray Caldwell (20-10) and Sam Coveleski (24-14) head up the pitching staff. Player/manager Tris Speaker (.388, 107 RBI), Elmer Smith (.316, 103 RBI) and Larry Gardner (.310, 118 RBI) lead the hitting attack.
[Note: Cleveland shortstop Ray Chapman is struck in the head with a pitched ball (from New York pitcher Carl Mays) and dies the next day. He is the major league's first and only game-related fatality.]

National League
The Brooklyn Dodgers (93-61) win their first pennant by 7 games over New York. Burleigh Grimes (23-11) is the ace of the Dodger pitching staff, which registers a 2.62 ERA. Zack Wheat (.328, 73 RBI) and Hy Meyers (.304, 80 RBI) pace the Brooklyn hitters.
[Note: Brooklyn and Boston play a 26-inning game, the longest ever (it is called because of darkness).]

WORLD SERIES

The Cleveland Indians win their 1st World Series, beating Brooklyn, 5 games to 2. Stan Coveleski's spitball pitching (2 earned runs over 27 innings) and Tris Speaker's bat (.320) are key factors. Coveleski wins all 3 games he starts (all 5-hitters). Elmer Smith is Cleveland's RBI leader (6), hitting the first grand-slam home run in Series history. Cleveland's Jim Bagby hits the first homer ever hit by a pitcher in Series play. Cleveland's Duster Mails, who is 7-0 during the regular season, pitches a shutout in game 6 to remain undefeated for the entire season.

AWARDS & HONORS

AL Pitching Leaders
Cleveland's pitching staff dominates the league, with Jim Bagby getting the most wins (31) and Stan Coveleski leading in strikeouts (133). Bob Shawkey (New York) has the lowest ERA (2.45). Chicago's Dickie Kerr and Urban Shocker (St. Louis) tie with the most saves (5). Walter Johnson (Washington) hurls the first and only no-hitter of his career.

AL Batting & Base Running Leaders
Ty Cobb (who is later named the new Detroit manager) loses the batting title for only the 2d time in the past 14 years as George Sisler (St. Louis) hits .407. Babe Ruth, who is now playing outfield full-time for New York, hits 54 homers and bats in 137, both new major league records. Sam Rice (Washington) is the stolen-base leader (63).

NL Pitching Leaders
Grover Cleveland Alexander (Chicago) again leads all NL pitchers with 1.91 ERA, 27 wins, and 173 strikeouts. Bill Sherdel is tops with 6 saves.

NL Batting & Base Running Leaders
Rogers Hornsby (St. Louis) wins his first batting title (.370) and also leads in RBI (94), hits (218) and doubles (44). Cy Williams (Philadelphia) slams 15 homers. Max Carey (Pittsburgh) leads in stolen bases (52) for the 6th time.

1921

REGULAR SEASON

American League
The New York Yankees (98-55), under manager Miller Huggins, win the first of many AL pennants. Babe Ruth, now an established slugger, sets several more records (see *Awards & Honors*). Bob Meusel (.318, 24 HRs, 135 RBI) and Wally Pipp (97 RBI) add to the potent Yankee lineup, which bangs out a record 134 home runs. Carl Mays (27-9) leads the pitching staff, which records 481 strikeouts and a league-best 3.79 ERA.

National League
The New York Giants (94-59) win the pennant (manager John McGraw's 7th) behind a potent offense headed by George Kelly (.308, 23 HRs, 122 RBI), Frankie Frisch (.341, 102 RBI) and Ross Youngs (.327, 102 RBI). Art Nehf (20-10) and Fred Toney (18-11) lead the pitching staff. The Giant defense completes 155 double plays, best in the NL.

WORLD SERIES

The first all-New York World Series ends with the Giants on top, 5 games to 3. Jesse Barnes and Phil Douglas win 2 games each as the Giants pound out 71 hits in support. George Burns (.333), Johnny Rawlings (.333) and Irish Meusel (.345), brother of the Yankees' Bob Meusel, all connect for 10 hits or more. Injuries keep Yankee star Babe Ruth out of the lineup for the last three games, but he does pick up his first Series home run in game 4.

AWARDS & HONORS

AL Pitching Leaders
Red Faber (Chicago) posts an ERA of 2.48. Carl Mays (New York) has the most wins (27, tied with Urban Shocker of St. Louis), and most saves (7, tied with Jim Middleton of Detroit). Walter Johnson (Washington) fans 143.

AL Batting & Base Running Leaders
Harry Heilmann (Detroit) hits .394 to better teammate Ty Cobb's .389 and collects 237 hits. Babe Ruth (New York) hits a record 59 home runs and drives home 171 runs. George Sisler (St. Louis) steals 35 bases.

NL Pitching Leaders
Burleigh Grimes (Brooklyn) has the most strikeouts (136) and ties Wilbur Cooper (Pittsburgh) for most wins (22). Bill Doak (St. Louis) has a 2.59 ERA and teammate Lou North earns 7 saves.

NL Batting & Base Running Leaders
Rogers Hornsby (St. Louis) again leads the NL in batting (.397), as well as hits (235), RBI (126), doubles (44) and triples (18, tied with Ray Powell of Boston). New York's George Kelly bangs out 23 home runs. Frankie Frisch (New York) takes the base-stealing crown (49).

1922

REGULAR SEASON

American League
The New York Yankees (94-60) squeeze past St. Louis by 1 game to repeat as AL champions. Bob Shawkey (20-12), Waite Hoyt (19-12) and Joe Bush (26-7) star on the mound. Babe Ruth (.315, 35 HRs, 99 RBI) and Wally Pipp (.329, 90 RBI) are the top hitters.

National League
The New York Giants (93-61) repeat as NL champions behind the hitting of George Kelly (.328, 107 RBI) and Irish Meusel (.331, 132 RBI). Pitching aces are Art Nehf (19-13) and Rosy Ryan (17-12). The Giants lead the league in fielding (.970) and in team ERA (3.45).

WORLD SERIES

The 2d straight all-New York Series (which returns to the original "best 4-out-of-7" format) ends in a sweep for the NL Giants, as their pitchers allow only 11 runs in 4 games. Jack Scott, a "sore arm" pitcher, limits the Yankees to 4 hits in game 3, and Art Nehf throws a 5-hitter in the clincher. Babe Ruth is held to only 2 hits in his 17 at-bats for the Series, and no Yankee gets more than 6 hits. Frankie Frisch (.471), Heinie Groh (.474) and Irish Meusel (7 RBI) lead the Giant offense.

AWARDS & HONORS

Most Valuable Players
AL: George Sisler (St. Louis)
NL: No selection

AL Pitching Leaders
Ed Rommel (Philadelphia) collects the most wins (27). Red Faber (Chicago) has the best ERA (2.80). Urban Shocker (St. Louis) leads in strikeouts (149). Sad Sam Jones (New York) registers 8 saves. Charlie Robertson (Chicago) hurls a perfect game against Detroit (April 30).

AL Batting Leaders
Detroit's Ty Cobb hits .401 but loses the batting title to George Sisler (St. Louis) who hits .420. Sisler also is tops with most runs scored (134) and most stolen bases (51). Ken Williams (St. Louis) belts 39 home runs and drives in 155 runs.

NL Pitching Leaders
Eppa Rixey (Cincinnati) wins 25 and Rosy Ryan (New York) leads in ERA (3.01). Dazzy Vance (Brooklyn) strikes out 134. Claude Jonnard's (New York) 5 saves top the league. Jesse Barnes (New York) throws a no-hitter.

NL Batting & Base Running Leaders
Rogers Hornsby (St. Louis) hits .401, smacks 42 HRs and collects 152 RBI, all league-leading totals, to win the Triple Crown. He also has most hits (250), doubles (46), runs scored (141) and total bases (450). Max Carey (Pittsburgh) grabs the base-stealing crown (51) for the 7th time.

REGULAR SEASON

American League
The New York Yankees (98-54) move into their new stadium and take the pennant for the 3d straight year, finishing 16 games ahead of Detroit. Babe Ruth (.393, 41 HRs, 131 RBI), Bob Meusel (.313, 91 RBI) and Wally Pipp (.304, 108 RBI) are the main offensive weapons. The mound corps, headed by Herb Pennock (19-6), Joe Bush (19-15) and Sad Sam Jones (21-8), posts a team ERA of 3.66.

National League
The New York Giants (95-58) keep pace with the Yankees and capture the pennant for the 3d straight year. Irish Meusel (19 HRs, 125 RBI), George Kelly (.307, 103 RBI) and Frankie Frisch (.348, 111 RBI) lead a powerful offense. Each of the 7 Giant pitchers, led by Rosy Ryan (16-5) and Jack Scott (16-7), end the season with a winning percentage over .500.

WORLD SERIES

In the 3d consecutive all-New York World Series, the Yankees avenge two previous defeats, beating the Giants, 4 games to 2. Herb Pennock stars on the mound with 2 wins, and Babe Ruth smacks 3 home runs. Irish Meusel (Giants) and brother Bob (Yankees) each get 7 hits, but Bob drives in 8 runs to lead his club. Casey Stengel of the Giants hits an inside-the-park homer in the 9th to win game 1, then robs Babe Ruth of his 3d home-run attempt in game 2 with a sensational catch, and finally smacks another homer to win game 3. Aaron Ward (Yankees) and Frankie Frisch (Giants) each rap out 10 hits in the Series.

AWARDS & HONORS

Most Valuable Players
AL: George Sisler (St. Louis)
NL: No selection

AL Pitching Leaders
George Uhle (Cleveland) hurls the most wins (26), and teammate Stan Coveleski has the best ERA (2.76). Walter Johnson (Washington), now in his 17th year in the majors, leads in strikeouts (130). Allan Russell (Washington) has a league-high 9 saves. Sam Jones (New York) and Howard Ehmke (Boston) both twirl no-hitters.

AL Batting & Base Running Leaders
Babe Ruth (New York) collects a record 170 walks and still leads the AL in RBI (130, tied with Tris Speaker of Cleveland), home runs (41) and runs scored (151). Harry Heilmann (Detroit) wins the batting title (.403) and Eddie Collins (Chicago) steals 47 bases.

NL Pitching Leaders
Dolf Luque (Cincinnati) wins 27 games, and has the lowest ERA (1.93). Dazzy Vance (Brooklyn) records 197 strikeouts. Claude Jonnard saves 5 games for New York.

NL Batting & Base Running Leaders
Rogers Hornsby (St. Louis) wins his 4th batting title (.384). Cy Williams (Philadelphia) hits 41 home runs and Irish Meusel (New York) collects 125 RBI. Max Carey (Pittsburgh) steals 51 bases.

The first ever Opening Day at **Yankee Stadium,** the "House that Ruth Built" (April 18).

REGULAR SEASON

American League
The Washington Senators (92-62) upset the champion New York Yankees, clinching the pennant by 2 games. Walter Johnson (23-7), in the twilight of his great career, leads the pitching corps. Goose Goslin (.344, 129 RBI) paces the hitters.

National League
The New York Giants (93-60) win their 4th straight pennant (John McGraw's 10th). George Kelly (.324, 136 RBI) and Irish Meusel (.310, 102 RBI) provide the power, as the Giant offense generates 95 home runs and a .300 team batting average. Art Nehf (14-4), Jack Bentley (16-5) and Virgil Barnes (16-10) head the pitching corps.

New York Yankee slugger **Babe Ruth** watches another home run sail into the stands. Ruth's 714 home runs stand as the major league record for 38 years. © National Baseball Library.

WORLD SERIES

The Washington Senators upset the New York Giants in a thrilling 7-game Series. Goose Goslin's 3 home runs and Tom Zachary's pitching (4 earned runs in 17⅔ innings) lead the Senators. Player/manager Bucky Harris (.333) drives in 7 runs for Washington. Walter Johnson, in his first World Series after 18 years with Washington, fans 12 but loses the opening game. He loses again in game 4 when the Giants erupt for 3 runs in the 9th inning. In game 7, Early McNeeley's bad-hop hit in the 12th inning wins the Series for Washington, giving Johnson credit for his first Series win (in relief).

AWARDS & HONORS

Most Valuable Players
AL: Walter Johnson (Washington)
NL: Dazzy Vance (Brooklyn)

AL Pitching Leaders
Walter Johnson (Washington) dominates AL pitchers with the most wins (23) and strikeouts (158) and the lowest ERA (2.72). Teammate Firpo Marberry picks up 17 saves.

AL Batting & Base Running Leaders
Babe Ruth (New York) bats .378 and belts 46 homers. Goose Goslin (Washington) leads in RBI (129). Eddie Collins (Chicago) leads in stolen bases with 42.

NL Pitching Leaders
Dazzy Vance (Brooklyn) leads the NL in wins (28), strikeouts (262) and ERA (2.16). Jakie May (Cincinnati) leads with 6 saves. Jesse Haines (St. Louis) tosses a no-hitter.

NL Batting & Base Running Leaders
Rogers Hornsby (St. Louis) hits for his all-time best average (.424). He also leads the league with 227 hits. Jake Fournier (Brooklyn) leads the home-run derby with 27 and George Kelly (New York) has the most RBI (136). Kiki Cuyler (32), Pie Traynor (24) and Max Carey (49), all from Pittsburgh, steal a total of 105 bases.

REGULAR SEASON

American League
The Washington Senators (96-55) repeat as AL champions behind the strong pitching of Stan Coveleski (20-5), Walter Johnson (20-7) and Dutch Ruether (18-7). Goose Goslin (.334, 113 RBI) and Sam Rice (.350, 87 RBI) lead the Washington hitting attack.

National League
The Pittsburgh Pirates (95-58) defeat the champion New York Giants by 8½ games behind a strong hitting attack (.307 team batting average) led by Pie Traynor (.320, 106 RBI), Glenn Wright (.308, 121 RBI), Clyde Barnhart (.325, 114 RBI) and Kiki Cuyler (.357, 102 RBI). Lee Meadows (19-10) and Ray Kremer (17-8) are the mound stars.

Two-time Triple Crown-winner **Rogers Hornsby** swings a mean bat for the St. Louis Cardinals. His career batting average of .359 remains 2d highest in baseball history.

WORLD SERIES

The Pittsburgh Pirates win the last 3 games of a dramatic 7-game Series to beat the Washington Senators. Ray Kremer and Vic Aldridge each win 2 games on the mound for Pittsburgh. Walter Johnson also wins 2 games, but in a losing cause for the Senators. Max Carey (.458) connects for 11 hits, steals 3 bases and scores 6 runs for the Pirates. Sam Rice (.364) and Joe Harris (.440) lead the Senators attack. In the 7th and deciding game, Pittsburgh comes from behind with a 13-hit attack to beat Johnson and win its first world championship since 1909.

AWARDS & HONORS

Most Valuable Players
AL: Roger Peckinpaugh (Washington)
NL: Rogers Hornsby (St. Louis)

AL Pitching Leaders
Stan Coveleski's (Washington) 2.84 ERA is best in the league. Rookie Lefty Grove (Philadelphia) leads in strikeouts (116). Ed Rommel (Philadelphia) and Ted Lyons (Chicago) tie for most wins (21). Firpo Marberry (Washington) earns 15 saves.

AL Batting & Base Running Leaders
Harry Heilmann (Detroit) wins the batting title for the 3d time (.393). Bob Muesel (New York) smacks 33 homers and raps out the most RBI (138). Johnny Mostil (Chicago) is the top base stealer (43).

NL Pitching Leaders
Dazzy Vance (Brooklyn) leads all pitchers with 22 wins and 221 strikeouts. He also pitches a no-hitter vs. Philadelphia. Dolf Luque's ERA (2.63) is lowest in the NL. Pittsburgh's Johnny Morrison and Guy Bush (Chicago) each gain 4 saves.

NL Batting & Base Running Leaders
Rogers Hornsby wins the Triple Crown for the 2d time on the strength of his batting average (403), plus 39 home runs and 143 RBI. Max Carey (Pittsburgh) is the #1 base stealer (46) for the 10th time in the past 13 years.

1926

REGULAR SEASON

American League
The New York Yankees (91-63) return as AL champions, finishing 3 games ahead of Cleveland. Their offense is led by a "Murderers Row" of Lou Gehrig (.313, 107 RBI), Babe Ruth (.372, 47 HRs, 145 RBI), Tony Lazzeri (114 RBI) and Bob Meusel (.315, 81 RBI). The pitching aces are Herb Pennock (23-11), Urban Shocker (19-11) and Waite Hoyt (16-12).

National League
The St. Louis Cardinals (89-65) nose out Cincinnati by 2 games to win the pennant. Their pitching staff is led by Flint Rehm (20-7), Jesse Haines (13-4) and Bill Sherdel (16-12). Jim Bottomley (.299, 120 RBI), Rogers Hornsby (.317, 93 RBI) and Les Bell (.325, 100 RBI) lead the offense.

WORLD SERIES

The St. Louis Cardinals, led by 16-year veteran pitcher Grover Cleveland Alexander, beat the New York Yankees, 4 games to 3. Cardinal batters Jim Bottomley (.345), Billy Southworth (.345) and Tommy Thevenow each connect for 10 hits. Alexander (0.89 ERA) and Jesse Haines (1.08 ERA) win 2 games apiece for the Cardinals. Three Yankee errors in the 7th game are key factors. Earle Combs (.357) and Babe Ruth (.300, 4 HRs) are the Yankee hitting stars (Ruth hits a record-breaking 3 home runs in game 4).

AWARDS & HONORS

Most Valuable Players
AL: George Burns (Cleveland)
NL: Bob O'Farrell (St. Louis)

AL Pitching Leaders
Lefty Grove's (Philadelphia) ERA (2.51) and 194 strikeouts head the pitching list. George Uhle (Cleveland) has the most wins (27). Firpo Marberry (Washington) sets a new record with 22 saves. Ted Lyons (Chicago) throws a no-hitter at the Red Sox.

AL Batting & Base Running Leaders
Heinie Manush (Detroit) beats out Babe Ruth for the batting crown (.378 to .372). Ruth (New York) hits 47 home runs and drives in 145. Johnny Mostil (Chicago) leads in stolen bases (35).

NL Pitching Leaders
Ray Kremer (Pittsburgh) leads the NL with 2.61 ERA and most wins (20, tied with 3 others). Brooklyn's Dazzy Vance repeats as strikeout king (140). New York's Chick Davies earns the most saves (6).

NL Batting & Base Running Leaders
Bubbles Hargrave (Cincinnati) takes the batting title (.353). Jim Bottomley (St. Louis) leads in RBI (120) and Hack Wilson (Chicago) belts 21 homers. Kiki Cuyler (Pittsburgh) captures the stolen-base crown from ex-teammate Max Carey (traded to Brooklyn) with 35.

1927

REGULAR SEASON

American League
A powerhouse New York Yankee team (110-44) overwhelms the rest of the league, winning by 19 games. Babe Ruth (.356, 60 HRs, 164 RBI) and Lou Gehrig (.373, 47 HRs, 175 RBI) are the slugging stars. Tony Lazzeri and Bob Meusel also drive in over 100 runs each. Waite Hoyt (22-7), Wilcy Moore (19-7, 13 saves), Herb Pennock (19-8) and Urban Shocker (18-6) form a solid pitching staff (3.20 team ERA).

National League
The Pittsburgh Pirates (94-60) win the pennant by 1½ games over St. Louis and 2 over New York. Ray Kremer (19-8), Lee Meadows (19-10) and Carmen Hill (22-11) head up the pitching corps. Paul Waner (.380, 131 RBI), Pie Traynor (.342, 106 RBI) and Glenn Wright (105 RBI) supply the offensive punch.

WORLD SERIES

The mighty New York Yankees sweep their Series against Pittsburgh, 4 games to 0. Babe Ruth (.400, 2 HRs, 7 RBI), Mark Koenig (.500) and Lou Gehrig (.308, 5 RBI) are also heavy hitters. The pitching staff posts a combined 2.00 ERA as Wilcy Moore, Herb Pennock, George Pipgras and Waite Hoyt each earn complete game victories. Lloyd Waner (.400) scores 5 runs to account for half of Pittsburgh's total.

AWARDS & HONORS

Most Valuable Player
AL: Lou Gehrig (New York)
NL: Paul Waner (Pittsburgh)

AL Pitching Leaders
Yankee pitching ace Waite Hoyt racks up the most wins (22, tied with Ted Lyons of Chicago) and lowest ERA (2.63). Lefty Grove (Chicago) repeats as strikeout ace (174). Washington's Garland Braxton ties Wilcy Moore (New York) with 13 saves.

AL Batting & Base Running Leaders
Babe Ruth (New York) hits a record 60 home runs and Lou Gehrig drives home a record 175. Detroit's Harry Heilmann captures his 4th batting title (.398). George Sisler (St. Louis) steals 27 bases to lead the league.

NL Pitching Leaders
Ray Kremer's (Pittsburgh) 2.47 ERA is tops in the NL. Charlie Root (Chicago) chalks up the most wins (26) and Dazzy Vance (Brooklyn) repeats as the league's strikeout king (184). Bill Sherdel (St. Louis) collects a league-high 6 saves.

NL Batting & Base Running Leaders
Paul Waner's (Pittsburgh) .380 average, 237 hits and 131 RBI lead all NL hitters. Cy Williams (Philadelphia) and Hack Wilson (Chicago) tie for most home runs with 30. Kiki Cuyler (Pittsburgh) retains his stolen-base title (35).

The mighty **New York Yankees** win 110 games during the regular season and sweep the Pirates in the 1927 World Series.

1928

American League

The New York Yankees (101-53) recapture the flag, but only by 2½ games over the Philadelphia A's. George Pipgras (24-13), Waite Hoyt (23-7) and Herb Pennock (17-6) lead the pitching staff. Babe Ruth (.323, 54 HRs, 142 RBI), Lou Gehrig (.374, 142 RBI) and Bob Meusel (.297, 113 RBI) lead the offense to a .450 team slugging average and 133 homers.

National League

The St. Louis Cardinals (95-59) take the pennant by 2 games over the New York Giants. Jesse Haines (20-8), Grover Cleveland Alexander (16-9), now in his 18th year, and Bill Sherdel (21-10) are the pitching mainstays. Jim Bottomley (.325, 31 HRs, 136 RBI) and Chick Hafey (.337, 27 HRs, 111 RBI) lead the offense.

The New York Yankees sweep the Series for the 2d year in a row, beating the St. Louis Cardinals 4 games to 0. Waite Hoyt picks up 2 wins, and Tom Zachary and George Pipgras one each, for a combined 2.00 ERA. Lou Gehrig (.545) paces the attack with 9 RBI and 4 home runs. Babe Ruth (.625) smacks 3 homers and scores 9 times. No Cardinal gets more than 5 hits and 29 go down on strikes during the one-sided Series.

Most Valuable Player

AL: Mickey Cochrane (Detroit)
NL: Jim Bottomley (St. Louis)

AL Pitching Leaders

Lefty Grove (Philadelphia) picks up the most wins (24, tied with George Pipgras of New York) and the most strikeouts (183). Garland Braxton (Washington) has the best ERA (2.51). New York's Waite Hoyte earns 8 saves.

AL Batting & Base Running Leaders

Babe Ruth (New York) clouts 54 homers and ties teammate Lou Gehrig for the RBI crown (142). Goose Goslin (Washington) wins the AL batting title (.379). Buddy Myer (Washington) is the stolen-base leader (30).

NL Pitching Leaders

Dazzy Vance (Brooklyn) fans 200 to lead all NL pitchers for the 7th year in a row. He also posts the best ERA (2.09). Larry Benton (New York) has the most wins (25, tied with Burleigh Grimes of Pittsburgh). Bill Sherdel and Hal Haid (both of St. Louis) collect 5 saves each.

NL Batting & Base Running Leaders

Rogers Hornsby (now with Boston) wins the batting title (.387). Jim Bottomley (St. Louis) drives in 136 runs and ties Hack Wilson (Chicago) for most HRs (31). Kiki Cuyler (now with Chicago) wins the stolen-base crown (37).

REGULAR SEASON

American League

Connie Mack's Philadelphia A's (104-46) coast to the AL pennant by 18 games over New York, as the Yankees' pitching staff falters. The A's Lefty Grove (20-6), Rube Walberg (18-11) and George Earnshaw (24-8) carry the pitching load for the Athletics. Al Simmons (.365, 34 HRs, 157 RBI), Jimmy Foxx (.354, 33 HRs, 117 RBI), Mickey Cochrane (.331, 95 RBI) and Bing Miller (.335, 93 RBI) lead the A's on offense. Philadelphia's defense commits the fewest errors in the majors (146).

National League

The Chicago Cubs (98-54), managed by Joe McCarthy, win the NL pennant by 10½ games over Pittsburgh. Good pitching from Charlie Root (19-6), Pat Malone (22-10) and Guy Bush (18-7), plus the NL's best defense (.975, 154 errors, and 169 double plays), are keys to the Cubs' success. Hack Wilson (.345, 39 HRs, 159 RBI), Kiki Cuyler (.360, 102 RBI) and Rogers Hornsby (.380, 39 HRs, 149 RBI) lead a powerful offense that generates 982 runs during the season.

WORLD SERIES

Philadelphia's home-run power is too much for the Chicago Cubs, who lose the Series 4 games to 1. Jimmy Foxx, Al Simmons and Mule Haas each hit 2 home runs for the A's (including a grand slam by Foxx in game 1) and account for 16 RBI. Jimmy Dykes (.421) collects 8 hits. George Earnshaw, Howard Ehmke, Rube Walberg and Ed Rommel each earn a win (Earnshaw's 13 strikeouts in game 1 represent a new Series record). Chicago's only win (game 3) is the National League's first in the last 11 Series games. In game 4, Philadelphia sends 10 runs across the plate to rally from an 8-0 deficit.

Connie Mack leads his Philadelphia Athletics to their first pennant since 1914. Mack's professional career spans 67 years, from 1883 as a minor league catcher to 1950, when he retires as president and manager of the Athletics.

AWARDS & HONORS

Most Valuable Players
AL: No selection
NL: Rogers Hornsby (Chicago)

AL Pitching Leaders
Lefty Grove (Philadelphia) has the lowest ERA (2.81) and the most strikeouts (170). Teammate George Earnshaw posts the most wins (24). Firpo Marberry (Washington) earns 11 saves.

AL Batting & Base Running Leaders
Lew Fonseca (Cleveland) beats out Al Simmons (Philadelphia) for the batting title (.369 to .365). Babe Ruth (New York) slams 46 home runs (including the 500th of his career, an all-time record), but loses his RBI crown to Al Simmons (157 to 154). Charlie Gehringer (Detroit) steals 28 bases.

NL Pitching Leaders
Pat Malone's (Chicago) 22 wins (including 5 shutouts) and 166 strikeouts are league highs. Bill Walker (New York) compiles the best ERA (3.09). Brooklyn's Johnny Morrison ties Guy Bush (Chicago) with 8 saves. Carl Hubbell (New York) tosses a no-hitter against Pittsburgh.

NL Batting & Base Running Leaders
Lefty O'Doul (Philadelphia) wins the batting crown (.398) and teammate Chuck Klein clouts 43 home runs. Hack Wilson (Chicago) drives in 159 runs and teammate Kiki Cuyler leads in stolen bases (43) for the 3d time in 4 years.

REGULAR SEASON

American League
Philadelphia (102-52) repeats its winning season of 1929, finishing 8 games in front of Washington. Lefty Grove (28-5) and George Earnshaw (22-13) are the mound stars. Jimmy Foxx (.335, 37 HRs, 156 RBI), Al Simmons (.381, 36 HRs, 165 RBI) and Bing Miller (.303, 100 RBI) again lead the powerful A's offense. On defense, Philadelphia is #1 in the league, committing only 145 errors.

National League
The St. Louis Cardinals (92-62) squeeze past the defending champion Chicago Cubs to take the flag by 2 games. While no Cardinal pitcher wins more than 15 games, the mound staff leads the NL in strikeouts (641) and saves (21). Frankie Frisch (.346, 114 RBI), rookie George Watkins (.373, 17 HRs, 87 RBI) and Chick Hafey (.336, 26 HRs, 107 RBI) supply the power on offense, which produces 1,004 runs (first team ever to score more than 1,000 runs in one season).

WORLD SERIES

Connie Mack's Philadelphia A's win another World Series, beating St. Louis 4 games to 2 with superior pitching (1.73 ERA and only 11 walks in 6 games) and the long ball (6 HRs). Al Simmons (.364) and Mickey Cochrane belt 2 homers each. George Earnshaw (0.72 ERA) and Lefty Grove (1.42 ERA) win 2 games apiece. Charley Gelbert (.353) is the only Cardinal to bat over .300. Teammate Chick Hafey bangs out 5 doubles in a losing cause.

AWARDS & HONORS

Most Valuable Players
No selections are made in 1930.

AL Pitching Leaders
Philadelphia's Lefty Grove carries off most of the pitching honors, including most wins (28), most strikeouts (209), best ERA (2.54) and most saves (9).

AL Batting & Base Running Leaders
Al Simmons (Philadelphia) noses out Lou Gehrig (New York) to win his first batting title (.381 to .379). Babe Ruth (New York) smacks 49 homers, while Gehrig picks up the most RBI (174). Marty McManus (Detroit) steals 23 bases.

NL Pitching Leaders
Dazzy Vance (Brooklyn) compiles the league's best ERA (2.61). Pat Malone (Chicago) and Ray Kremer (Pittsburgh) tie for the most wins (20). Bill Hallahan (St. Louis) leads in strikeouts (177). Hi Bell (St. Louis) earns 8 saves.

NL Batting & Base Running Leaders
Bill Terry (New York) grabs the batting crown (.401) and has the most hits (254). Hack Wilson (Chicago) clouts 56 HRs (an NL record) and collects a major league record 190 RBI. Kiki Cuyler (Chicago) is the base-stealing champ (37) for the 3d straight year.

The heavy hitting of (l. to r.) **Mickey Cochrane, Al Simmons, Mule Haas, Jimmy Foxx** and **Bing Miller** leads the Philadelphia Athletics to three straight World Series (1929–1931).

1931

REGULAR SEASON

American League
The Philadelphia A's (107-45) win their 3d straight pennant, finishing 13½ games in front of the New York Yankees. A strong pitching staff, led by Lefty Grove (31-4), George Earnshaw (21-7) and Rube Walberg (20-12), registers 97 complete games and 12 shutouts to lead the AL. Power hitting by Jimmy Foxx (30 HRs, 120 RBI) and Al Simmons (.390, 22 HRs, 128 RBI) again keys the offense.

National League
The St. Louis Cardinals (101-53) retain the NL championship by a 13-game margin over New York. Rookie pitcher Paul Derringer (18-8) leads the pitching staff along with veterans Burleigh Grimes (17-9), Jesse Haines (12-3) and Bill Hallahan (19-9). Chick Hafey (.349, 95 RBI), Frankie Frisch (.311, 82 RBI) and Jim Bottomley (.348) are the Cards' top hitters.

WORLD SERIES

The St. Louis Cardinals, dubbed "the gas house gang" for their fiery style of play, avenge their 1930 Series defeat, beating Philadelphia 4 games to 3. Bill Hallahan (2 earned runs in 18⅓ innings) and Burleigh Grimes win 2 games apiece. Pepper Martin, Cardinal outfielder, gets 12 hits, good for 5 RBI and a .500 average. Jimmy Foxx (.348) and Al Simmons (.333, 2 HRs, 8 RBI) lead the A's offense. Lefty Grove wins 2 games in a losing cause. In game 7, Philadelphia scores 2 runs in the 9th but falls 1 short of tying the game.

AWARDS & HONORS

Most Valuable Players
AL: Lefty Grove (Philadelphia)
NL: Frankie Frisch (St. Louis)

AL Pitching Leaders
Lefty Grove (Philadelphia) wins all the pitching honors with most wins (31), most strikeouts (175) and best ERA (2.06). Wilcy Moore (Boston) earns 10 saves. Wes Ferrell (Cleveland) and Bob Burke (Washington) pitch no-hitters during the season.

AL Batting & Base Running Leaders
New York Yankee teammates Babe Ruth and Lou Gehrig tie for the HR crown with 46, though Gehrig leads in RBI (184). Al Simmons (Philadelphia) repeats as the batting champ (.390) and Ben Chapman (New York) steals 61 bases.

NL Pitching Leaders
Bill Hallahan (St. Louis) wins 19 games and strikes out 159. Bill Walker (New York) has the best ERA (2.26). Jack Quinn (Brooklyn) registers 15 saves.

NL Batting & Base Running Leaders
Bill Terry (New York) and Chick Hafey (St. Louis) tie for the NL batting championship (.349). Chuck Klein (Philadelphia) belts 31 home runs and drives in 121. Frankie Frisch (St. Louis) leads in steals with 28.

1932

REGULAR SEASON

American League
The New York Yankees (107-47) regain the AL championship after a 3-year Philadelphia reign. Lefty Gomez (24-7), Johnny Allen (17-4) and Red Ruffing (18-7) are the new pitching stars in support of veteran George Pipgras (16-9). Babe Ruth (.341, 41 Hrs, 137 RBI), Lou Gehrig (.349, 34 HRs, 151 RBI), Tony Lazzeri (.300, 107 RBI) and Ben Chapman (.299, 107 RBI) lead the mighty offense, which generates 1,002 runs (only the 2d time a team has scored over 1,000 runs in one season).

National League
The Chicago Cubs (90-64) finish ahead of the NL pack by 4 games over Pittsburgh. Rookie pitcher Lon Warneke (22-6) joins a veteran staff (3.44 team ERA) of Guy Bush (19-11), Pat Malone (15-17) and Charlie Root (15-10). Riggs Stephenson (.324) and Babe Herman (.314) are the top hitters on this weak-hitting squad.

WORLD SERIES
Joe McCarthy's New York Yankees maul the Chicago Cubs, 4 games to 0, as Chicago's pitching staff gives up 37 runs. Lou Gehrig (3 HRs, 8 RBI), Babe Ruth (.333, 2 HRs, 6 RBI), Bill Dickey (.438) and Tony Lazzeri (5 RBI) are responsible for most of the damage. In game 3, Ruth makes baseball history by pointing to stands moments before he slams a homer in the same spot. Lefty Gomez, Red Ruffing, George Pipgras and Wilcy Moore win 1 game apiece for New York (Herb Pennock is credited with 2 saves).

AWARDS & HONORS

Most Valuable Players
AL: Jimmy Foxx (Philadelphia)
NL: Chuck Klein (Philadelphia)

AL Pitching Leaders
General Crowder (Washington) chalks up 26 wins. Red Ruffing (New York) registers 190 strikeouts. Lefty Grove's (Philadelphia) 2.84 ERA is tops, and Firpo Marberry (Washington) again leads the league with 13 saves.

AL Batting & Base Running Leaders
Jimmy Foxx (Philadelphia) leads the league in home runs (58) and RBI (169). Dale Alexander (Detroit/Boston) wins the batting crown (.367). Ben Chapman (New York) takes base-stealing honors with 38 thefts.

NL Pitching Leaders
Rookie Lon Warneke (Chicago) has the most wins (22) and the lowest ERA (2.37). Dizzy Dean (St. Louis), another oustanding rookie, records the most strikeouts (191). Jack Quinn (Brooklyn) earns 8 saves to lead the league.

NL Batting & Base Running Leaders
Mel Ott (New York) and Chuck Klein (Philadelphia) each hit 38 homers. Klein has the most hits (226), most stolen bases (20), and scores the most runs (152). Don Hurst (Philadelphia) drives home 143 runs.

1933

REGULAR SEASON

American League
The Washington Senators (99-53) upset the defending champion New York Yankees, winning the pennant by 7 games. General Crowder (24-15), Earl Whitehill (22-8) and Jack Russell (12-6) are the aces of Washington's unheralded pitching staff, which records 26 saves and walks only 452. Player/manager Joe Cronin (.309, 118 RBI), Joe Kuhel (.322, 107 RBI) and Heinie Manush (.336, 95 RBI) lead the hitting attack.

National League
The New York Giants (91-61) win their first NL flag since 1924, beating out the Pittsburgh Pirates by 5 games. Carl Hubbell (23-12) is the new ace of New York's pitching staff, which includes Hal Schumacher (19-12) and "Fat Freddie" Fitzsimmons (16-11). Mel Ott (23 HRs, 103 RBI) and player/manager Bill Terry (.322) pace the offense.

ALL-STAR GAME & WORLD SERIES

All-Star Game (Chicago, AL)
In the first All-Star game, the AL defeats the NL, 4-2. Babe Ruth (New York) belts a dramatic home run in the 3d inning to lead the AL.

World Series
The New York Giants defeat the Washington Senators, 4 games to 1, behind the pitching of Carl Hubbell (2-0), who allows no earned runs in 20 innings of work. Mel Ott (.389, 2 HRs) and Kiddo Davis (.368) pace the hitting attack. Earl Whitehill salvages the only game (#3) for Washington with a 5-hit shutout. Fred Schulte (.333, 4 RBI) is the leading batter for Washington.

AWARDS & HONORS

Most Valuable Players
AL: Jimmy Foxx (Philadelphia)
NL: Carl Hubbell (New York)

AL Pitching Leaders
Lefty Grove (Philadelphia) and General Crowder (Washington) tie for the most wins (24). Lefty Gomez (New York) also strikes out 163 and Monte Pearson (Cleveland) turns in the lowest ERA (2.33). Jack Russell (Washington) saves 13 games.

AL Batting & Base Running Leaders
Jimmy Foxx (Philadelphia) wins the Triple Crown with 48 home runs, 163 RBI and a .356 batting average (tied with Heinie Manush of Washington). Ben Chapman (New York) keeps his stolen-base title (27).

NL Pitching Leaders
Carl Hubbell (New York) wins 23 games, including 10 shutouts, and his ERA (1.66) is the lowest among all pitchers in almost 15 years. Dizzy Dean (St. Louis) strikes out 199. Phil Collins saves 6 games for Philadelphia.

NL Batting & Base Running Leaders
Chuck Klein (Philadelphia) leads in HRs (28), RBI (120), hits (223) and batting average (.368), earning him the Triple Crown. Pepper Martin (St. Louis) is #1 in stolen bases (26) and runs scored (122).

Pitchers (l. to r.) **Hal Schumacher, Carl Hubbell** and **Freddie Fitzsimmons** of the 1933 World Series champion New York Giants. © AP

REGULAR SEASON

American League

The Detroit Tigers (101-53) win their first pennant since 1909, finishing 7 games ahead of New York. Schoolboy Rowe (24-8), Eldon Auker (15-7) and Tommy Bridges (22-11) lead the Tiger pitching staff. The AL's best hitting team (.300 team average) features Hank Greenberg (.339, 26 HRs, 139 RBI), Charlie Gehringer (.356, 127 RBI) and Goose Goslin (.305, 100 RBI).

National League

St. Louis (95-58) captures its 5th pennant in the last 9 years, narrowly edging the Giants by 2 games. Cardinal pitching stars are Dizzy Dean (30-7) and his brother Paul (19-11), who lead a staff that produces 689 strikeouts and 78 complete games. Rip Collins (.333, 35 HRs, 128 RBI) and Joe "Ducky" Medwick (.319, 106 RBI) star on offense.

At the Polo Grounds in New York, St. Louis Cardinal second baseman **Frankie Frisch** touches home plate after blasting a home run in the 2d All–Star game (July 10). © UPI

ALL-STAR GAME & WORLD SERIES

All-Star Game (New York, NL)

The AL outscores the NL, 9-7, but the heroics belong to NL pitcher Carl Hubbell (New York) who strikes out superstars Babe Ruth (New York), Lou Gehrig (New York), Jimmy Foxx (Philadelphia), Al Simmons (Chicago) and Joe Cronin (Washington) in succession.

World Series

The St. Louis Cardinals win an exciting 7-game Series behind the pitching of the Dean brothers: Dizzy (2 wins, 17 strikeouts) and Paul (2 wins, 11 strikeouts). Pepper Martin (.355, 8 runs scored), Rip Collins (.367) and Joe "Ducky" Medwick (.379) are the heavy hitters. In game 7, the Cardinals score 7 runs in the 3d inning to put the game—and Series—on ice. Joe Medwick is ordered out of the game in the 6th inning by baseball commissioner Landis as Detroit fans, angered by a fight between a Cardinal player and the Tigers' third baseman, pelt Medwick with debris.

AWARDS & HONORS

Most Valuable Players

AL: Mickey Cochrane (Detroit)
NL: Dizzy Dean (St. Louis)

AL Pitching Leaders

Lefty Gomez (New York) produces the lowest ERA (2.33), most wins (26) and most strikeouts (158). Bobo Newsom (Detroit) allows no hits for 9 innings against Boston, then loses the game in the 10th.

AL Batting & Base Running Leaders

Lou Gehrig (New York) slams 49 HRs, drives in 165, and bats .363 to lead with the Triple Crown. Billy Werber (Boston) steals 40 bases for the league title.

NL Pitching Leaders

Dizzy Dean (St. Louis) and Carl Hubbell (New York) share NL pitching honors. Dean has the most wins (30) and most strikeouts (195). Hubbell records a 2.30 ERA and earns the most saves (8). Paul "Daffy" Dean (Dizzy's brother) hurls a no-hitter against Brooklyn.

NL Batting & Base Running Leaders

Paul Waner's (Pittsburgh) batting average of .362 tops the NL. He also collects 217 hits and scores 122 runs. Mel Ott (New York) leads in HRs (35, tied with Rip Collins of St. Louis) and RBI (135). Pepper Martin (St.Louis) steals a league-high 23 bases.

REGULAR SEASON

American League
Detroit (93-58) captures its 2d AL flag in a row behind a solid 4-man pitching rotation featuring Tommy Bridges (21-10), Schoolboy Rowe (19-13), Eldon Auker (18-7) and General Crowder (16-10). Hank Greenberg's slugging (.328, 36 HRs, 170 RBI) and the steady hitting of Charlie Gehringer (.330, 108 RBI) and Goose Goslin (.292, 109 RBI) pace the Tiger attack.

National League
The Chicago Cubs (100-54) win the NL pennant only 4 games in front of St. Louis. Pitchers Lon Warneke (20-13) and Bill Lee (20-6) head up a solid mound corps (team ERA of 3.26 is lowest in the majors). Billy Herman (.341), Augie Galan (.314) and Gabby Hartnett (.344, 91 RBI) carry the offensive load.

ALL-STAR GAME & WORLD SERIES

All-Star Game (Cleveland, AL)
The AL wins its 3d All-Star game in a row, defeating the NL, 4-1. Jimmy Foxx (Philadelphia) drives in 3 runs with a 2-run homer and an RBI single to lead the AL.

World Series
The Detroit Tigers defeat Chicago Cubs, 4 games to 2, in a close, dramatic Series. Pete Fox (.385) and Charlie Gehringer (.375) are the batting stars for Detroit. Tommy Bridges wins 2 games, including the 6th game when Detroit scores the winning run in the bottom of the 9th. Billy Herman (.333, 6 RBI) is the only effective Chicago hitter.

AWARDS & HONORS

Most Valuable Players
AL: Hank Greenberg (Detroit)
NL: Gabby Hartnett (Chicago)

AL Pitching Leaders
Wes Ferrell (Boston) tops the AL in wins (25). Lefty Grove's (Boston) ERA (2.70) leads all pitchers. Tommy Bridges (Detroit) compiles the most strikeouts (163). Jack Knott saves 7 games for St. Louis. Vern Kennedy (Chicago) throws the year's only no-hitter in the major leagues.

AL Batting & Base Running Leaders
Hank Greenberg (Detroit) leads the league in home runs (36, ties Jimmy Foxx of Philadelphia) and RBI (170). Buddy Myer (Washington) narrowly wins the batting title over Joe Vosmik of Cleveland (.349 to .348). Billy Werber (Boston) retains the base-stealing crown (29).

NL Pitching Leaders
Cy Blanton (Pittsburgh) leads the pack with a .258 ERA. Dizzy Dean (St. Louis) racks up the most wins (28) and strikeouts (182). Brooklyn's Dutch Leonard is credited with a league-high 8 saves.

NL Batting & Base Running Leaders
Wally Berger (Cincinnati) blasts 34 homers and leads the league in RBI (130). Arky Vaughan (Pittsburgh) is the batting champion (.385). Augie Galan (Chicago) is the leader in stolen bases with 22.

1936

REGULAR SEASON

American League
The New York Yankees (102-51), in their 2d year without Babe Ruth (traded to Boston in the NL following the 1934 season), continue to dominate the league, finishing 19½ games in front of 2d-place Detroit. The team's home run total (182) is an all-time high, and the pitching staff's ERA (4.17) is lowest in the AL. Red Ruffing (20-12), Pat Malone (12-4, 9 saves) and Monte Pearson (19-7) are the mound aces, while Lou Gehrig (.354, 49 HRs, 152 RBI) and Joe DiMaggio (.323, 29 HRs, 125 RBI) are the big run producers.

National League
The New York Giants (92-62) finish ahead of Chicago and St. Louis by 5 games. Carl Hubbell (26-6) is the ace of the pitching staff, which leads the NL with a 3.46 ERA. Mel Ott (.328, 33 HRs, 135 RBI) is the major offensive weapon.

ALL-STAR GAME & WORLD SERIES

All-Star Game (Boston, NL)
The NL wins its first All-Star game, 4-3, behind the strong pitching of New York's Carl Hubbell and Dizzy Dean (St. Louis).

World Series
In the first "Subway Series" in New York since 1923, the Yankees defeat the Giants, 4 games to 2. The powerful Yankees attack is too much for the Giants' pitching staff, as Red Rolfe (.400), Joe DiMaggio (.346), Tony Lazzeri (7 RBI) and Lou Gehrig (2 HRs, 7 RBI) lead the way. New York breaks a Series record in game 2, scoring 18 runs (most ever in one Series game).

AWARDS & HONORS

Hall of Fame Inductees
Ty Cobb, Walter Johnson, Christy Mathewson, Babe Ruth and Honus Wagner.

Most Valuable Players
AL: Lou Gehrig (New York)
NL: Carl Hubbell (New York)

AL Pitching Leaders
Lefty Grove's (Boston) 2.81 ERA leads the AL. Tommy Bridges (Detroit) has the most wins (23) and most strikeouts (175). Pat Malone (New York) earns 9 saves.

AL Batting & Base Running Leaders
Lou Gehrig (New York) leads in HRs (49) while Hal Trosky (Cleveland) is the RBI leader (162). Luke Appling (Chicago) bats .388. Lyn Lary (St. Louis) is the stolen-base leader (37).

NL Pitching Leaders
Carl Hubbell's (New York) ERA (2.31) is best in the NL. He also leads in wins (26). Van Mungo (Brooklyn) has the most strikeouts (238). Dizzy Dean (St. Louis) saves 11 games.

NL Batting & Base Running Leaders
Paul Waner (Pittsburgh) wins his 2d batting title (.373). Mel Ott (New York) clouts 33 homers. Joe "Ducky" Medwick (St. Louis) drives home 138 runs, leads in doubles (64) and has the most hits (223). Pepper Martin (St. Louis) leads in stolen bases (23) for the 3d time in 4 years.

1937

REGULAR SEASON

American League
The New York Yankees (102-52) repeat as champions of the AL, finishing 13 games in front of Detroit. Lefty Gomez (21-11) and Red Ruffing (20-7) are the pitching leaders. Joe DiMaggio (.346, 46 HRs, 167 RBI), Bill Dickey (.332, 29 HRs, 133 RBI) and Lou Gehrig (.351, 37 HRs, 159 RBI) pace the powerful Yankee attack.

National League
The New York Giants (95-57) win easily to set up the 2d "Subway Series" in a row. Carl Hubbell (22-8) and Hal Schumacher (20-9) are the pitching mainstays. Mel Ott (.294, 31 HRs, 95 RBI) continues his heavy hitting as the Giant offense leads the NL with 111 home runs.

ALL-STAR GAME & WORLD SERIES

All-Star Game (Washington, AL)
The AL wins, 8-3, behind 4 RBI from New York's Lou Gehrig. Dizzy Dean (St. Louis) is injured by a line drive off his foot, which eventually results in a sore arm, forcing him out of baseball.

World Series
The New York Yankees retain their world championship, defeating the New York Giants, 4 games to 1. The Yankee pitchers, led by Red Ruffing (2-0), register a combined 2.45 ERA in the Series. Their offense outscores the Giants, 26 runs to 12. For the victorious Yanks, Joe Gordon (6 RBI) and Bill Dickey both bat .400, and Frank Crosetti drives home 6 runs.

AWARDS & HONORS

Hall of Fame Inductees
Nap Lajoie, Connie Mack, John Mc-Graw, Tris Speaker, George Wright, Cy Young

Most Valuable Players
AL: Charlie Gehringer (Detroit)
NL: Joe "Ducky" Medwick (St. Louis).

AL Pitching Leaders
Lefty Gomez (New York) has the best ERA (2.33), most wins (21) and most strikeouts (194). Johnny Allen (Cleveland) compiles a won-lost record of 15-1, setting a record for pitcher's winning percentage (.938). Clint Brown (Chicago) saves 18 games in relief. Bill Dietrich (Chicago) hurls the major league's only no-hitter for 1937.

AL Batting & Base Running Leaders
Joe DiMaggio (New York) slams 46 HRs. Hank Greenberg (Detroit) drives in 183 runs. His teammate, Charlie Gehringer, bats .371. Billy Werber (Philadelphia) and Ben Chapman (Boston/Washington) tie for the most stolen bases (35).

NL Pitching Leaders
Carl Hubbell (New York) posts the most wins (22) and strikeouts (159). Jim Turner (Boston) turns in the best ERA (2.38). Pittsburgh's Mace Brown ties Cliff Melton (New York) with 7 saves.

NL Batting & Base Running Leaders
Joe "Ducky" Medwick (St. Louis) wins the Triple Crown with a .374 batting average, 154 RBI and 31 homers (tied with New York's Mel Ott). Augie Galan (Chicago) steals the most bases (23) for the 2d time in 3 years.

Posing before the 1937 All–Star game at Washington's Griffith Stadium, each of these American League stars is eventually voted into the Hall of Fame: (l. to r.) **Lou Gehrig, Joe Cronin, Bill Dickey, Joe DiMaggio, Charlie Gehringer, Jimmy Foxx and Hank Greenberg.** © UPI

REGULAR SEASON

American League

The New York Yankees (99-53) win their 3d straight pennant, finishing 9½ games in front of Boston. Spud Chandler (14-5) joins a veteran pitching staff featuring Red Ruffing (21-7), Lefty Gomez (18-12) and Monte Pearson (16-7). The New York lineup blasts a total of 174 home runs. Lou Gehrig (.295, 29 HRs, 114 RBI), Joe Gordon (25 HRs, 97 RBI), Joe Di-Maggio (.324, 32 HRs, 140 RBI), and Bill Dickey (.313, 27 HRs, 115 RBI) are the chief run producers.

National League

The Chicago Cubs (89-63) sneak past Pittsburgh to take the NL flag by 2 games. Bill Lee (22-9) and Clay Bryant (19-11) lead a pitching staff which, with NL's lowest ERA (3.37), holds Chicago's opponents to the fewest runs (598). Stan Hack (.320) and Carl Reynolds (.302) are the big hitters on a weak-hitting club.

ALL-STAR GAME & WORLD SERIES

All-Star Game (Cincinnati, NL)

The NL, with good pitching from Cincinnati's Johnny "No-Hit" Vander Meer (see *Awards & Honors*) and Bill Lee (Chicago), sinks the AL, 4-1.

World Series

The New York Yankees sweep the Chicago Cubs, 4 games to 0, for their 3d straight world championship. New York's pitching staff, led by Red Ruffing (2 wins), Monte Pearson (1 win) and Lefty Gomez (1 win), fans 26 Cubs and allows only 9 runs for a combined ERA of 1.75. Frank Crosetti drives home 6 Yankees. Bill Dickey and Joe Gordon both hit .400 for New York.

AWARDS & HONORS

Hall of Fame Inductee

Grover Cleveland Alexander

Most Valuable Players

AL: Jimmy Foxx (Boston)
NL: Ernie Lombardi (Cincinnati)

AL Pitching Leaders

Red Ruffing (New York) wins 21 games. Bob Feller, Cleveland's fastballer, strikes out 240. Lefty Grove's (Boston) ERA (3.08) tops all AL hurlers. Johnny Murphy saves 11 games for New York. Yankee teammate Monte Pearson tosses a no-hitter.

AL Batting & Base Running Leaders

Jimmy Foxx (Boston) leads in batting average (.349) and RBI (175). Detroit slugger Hank Greenberg smashes 58 homers. Frank Crosetti (New York) leads in stolen bases (27).

NL Pitching Leaders

Bill Lee (Chicago) leads all NL pitchers in wins (22), ERA (2.66) and shutouts (9). Teammate Clay Bryant fans 135. Johnny "No-Hit" Vander Meer (Cincinnati) pitches 2 no-hit, no-run games in succession (June 11 and 15), a feat that has not been duplicated.

NL Batting & Base Running Leaders

Mel Ott (New York) slugs 36 HRs. Joe "Ducky" Medwick (St. Louis) drives in 122 runs. Ernie Lombardi (Cincinnati) wins the batting crown (.342). Stan Hack (Chicago) is the top base stealer (16).

In the first night game ever at Ebbets Field (June 15), Cincinnati's **Johnny "No–Hit" Vander Meer** hurls the 2d of his two consecutive no-hitters, a major league record. © AP

1939

REGULAR SEASON

American League
The New York Yankees (106-45) easily take the AL pennant for the 4th straight year, beating 2d place Boston by a whopping 17 games. Red Ruffing (21-7) and 6 other Yankee hurlers produce a 3.31 ERA, 26 saves, 12 shutouts and 87 complete games. Joe DiMaggio (.381, 30 HRs, 126 RBI) leads a powerful attack at the plate. On May 2, "Iron Man" Lou Gehrig takes himself out of the lineup after playing 2,130 consecutive games, a major league record. Gehrig dies in 1941 from an illness later known as "Lou Gehrig's" disease.

National League
Cincinnati (97-57) wins its first NL pennant since 1919, finishing 4½ games ahead of St. Louis. Bucky Walters (27-11) and Paul Derringer (25-7) star on the mound for the Reds. Frank McCormick (.332, 128 RBI) and Ernie Lombardi (20 HRs, 85 RBI) carry the heavy bats.

ALL-STAR GAME & WORLD SERIES

All-Star Game (New York, AL)
The AL wins, 3-1, with Bob Feller's (Cleveland) strong relief pitching and a 2-run, 4th inning rally featuring George Selkirk's (New York) run-producing single and an unearned run. Joe DiMaggio's (New York) homer in the 5th inning provides a cushion for the AL.

World Series
The New York Yankees complete their 2d straight sweep and gain their 8th world championship as pitchers Red Ruffing, Monte Pearson, Bump Hadley and Johnny Murphy each earn a victory. They hold Cincinnati hitters to a total of 8 earned runs and yield only 4 extra base hits for the Series. Charlie Keller (.438) clouts 3 home runs, knocks in 6 runs, and scores 8 times to lead the Yankee offense. Frank McCormick (.400) is the only Cincinnati batter to collect more than 5 hits in the Series.

AWARDS & HONORS

Hall of Fame Inductees
Eddie Collins, Lou Gehrig, Wee Willie Keeler, George Sisler
[Note: As part of baseball's centennial celebration in 1939, the following "Oldtimers" are honored: Cap Anson, Charles Comiskey, Candy Cummings, Buck Ewing, Charlie Radbourn, Albert Spalding.]

Most Valuable Players
AL: Joe DiMaggio (New York)
NL: Bucky Walters (Cincinnati)

AL Pitching Leaders
Bob Feller (Cleveland) wins 24 games and fans 246. Lefty Grove (Boston) posts the lowest ERA (2.54). Johnny Murphy (New York) is credited with 19 saves.

AL Batting & Base Running Leaders
Jimmy Foxx (Boston) leads the league in HRs (35). Joe DiMaggio (New York) is the batting champion (.381). Ted Williams, a rookie outfielder for Boston, drives in 145 runs and has the most total bases (344). George Case (Washington) is the new base-stealing champion (51).

NL Pitching Leaders
Bucky Walters (Cincinnati) wins 27 games and produces an ERA of 2.29 to lead the league. Claude Passeau (Chicago) ties Walters for most strikeouts (137). St. Louis teammates Bob Bowman and Clyde Shoun tie with 9 saves apiece.

NL Batting & Base Running Leaders
Johnny Mize (St. Louis) clouts 28 HRs and wins the batting title (.349). Frank McCormick (Cincinnati) leads in RBI (128) and hits (209). Stan Hack (Chicago) and Lee Handley (Pittsburgh) share the base-stealing crown (17).

Babe Ruth (r.) embraces his longtime teammate, **Lou Gehrig**, on "Lou Gehrig Day" at Yankee Stadium (July4). © UPI

REGULAR SEASON

American League
The Detroit Tigers (90-64) end the long Yankee reign, edging out Cleveland by 1 game and New York by 2. Pitchers Bobo Newsom (21-5) and Schoolboy Rowe (16-3) are the aces on a mound staff that amasses 752 strikeouts and 23 saves. Rudy York (.316, 33 HRs, 134 RBI) and Hank Greenberg (.340, 41 HRs, 150 RBI) lead a powerful Tiger attack.

National League
The Cincinnati Reds (100-53) repeat as NL champions, finishing 12 games in front of Brooklyn. Good pitching (3.05 team ERA) and fielding (117 errors) make up for the lack of fire power. Bucky Walters (22-10) and Paul Derringer (20-12) again head up the pitching corps. Frank McCormick (.309, 19 HRs, 127 RBI) and Ernie Lombardi (.319, 14 HRs, 74 RBI) are the Reds' only power hitters.

ALL-STAR GAME & WORLD SERIES

All-Star Game (St. Louis, NL)
The NL wins 4-0, the first shutout in All-Star game history, jumping on New York Yankee ace Red Ruffing for 3 runs in the 1st inning.

World Series
Cincinnati wins its first World Series, beating Detroit in a well-pitched 7-game Series. Paul Derringer (2-1) and Bucky Walters (2-0) throttle Detroit's heavy hitters. Billy Werber (.370), Mike McCormick (.310) and Ival Goodman (5 RBI, 5 runs scored) provide the Reds' batting power. Bobo Newsom (2-1, 1.38 ERA) stars on the mound for Detroit. Hank Greenberg (.357, 6 RBI), Pinky Higgins (.333, 6 RBI) and Bruce Campbell (.360, 5 RBI) lead the Tiger attack. The Reds score 2 runs in the 7th inning of the 7th and deciding game to capture their first world championship since the "Black Sox Scandal" of 1919.

AWARDS & HONORS

Hall of Fame Inductees
None

Most Valuable Players
AL: Hank Greenberg (Detroit)
NL: Frank McCormick (Cincinnati)

AL Pitching Leaders
Cleveland's Bob Feller wins 27 games, strikes out 261, and hurls a no-hitter against Chicago on opening day at Cleveland. Ernie Bonham (New York) has the best ERA (1.90). Al Benton (Detroit) records 17 saves.

AL Batting & Base Running Leaders
Joe DiMaggio (New York) wins the AL batting title for the 2d year in a row (.352). Hank Greenberg (Detroit) hits the most homers (41) and leads in RBI (150), total bases (384) and slugging (.670). Three men tie for the most hits (200). George Case (Washington) repeats as base-stealing champ with 35 thefts.

NL Pitching Leaders
Bucky Walters (Cincinnati) produces the best ERA (2.48) and most wins (22). Kirby Higbe (Philadelphia) strikes out 137. Tex Carleton (Brooklyn) tosses a no-hitter. Three pitchers top the league with 7 saves.

NL Batting & Base Running Leaders
Johnny Mize (St. Louis) leads all NL hitters with 43 HRs and 137 RBI. Debs Garms (Pittsburgh) wins the batting championship (.355). Lonny Frey (Cincinnati) steals a league-high 22 bases (one more than Stan Hack, whose 191 hits for Chicago ties Cincinnati's Frank McCormick).

1941

REGULAR SEASON

American League
The New York Yankees (101-53) regain the AL championship, their 5th in 6 years, winning by 17 games over 2d-place Boston. A well-balanced pitching staff (no member wins more than 15 games), good fielding (196 double plays) and solid hitting lead the way. Joe DiMaggio (.357, 30 HRs, 125 RBI), Joe Gordon (24 HRs, 87 RBI) and Charlie Keller (.298, 33 HRs, 122 RBI) all enjoy good years at bat.

National League
The Brooklyn Dodgers (100-54) win their first pennant since 1920. Kirby Higbe (22-9) and Whit Wyatt (22-10) are the club's outstanding pitchers. Dolf Camilli (.285, 34 HRs, 120 RBI), Joe "Ducky" Medwick (.318, 18 HRs, 88 RBI) and Pete Reiser (.343, 76 RBI) lead a strong offense that produces 101 home runs and 800 runs.

ALL-STAR GAME & WORLD SERIES

All-Star Game (Detroit, AL)
Ted Williams (Boston) hits a dramatic 9th inning 3-run homer with two outs and wins it for the AL 7-5. Arky Vaughan (Pittsburgh) sets an All-Star game record by slamming 2 home runs.

World Series
The New York Yankees win 4 games to 1 over the Brooklyn Dodgers, a low-scoring Series (only 28 runs are scored by both teams in 5 games). New York's pitchers have a combined ERA of 1.80 for the Series. Joe Gordon (.500, 5 RBI) and Charlie Keller (.389, 5 RBI) account for most of the Yankee offense. The defense commits only 2 errors in the 5-game Series, and no Dodger batter gets more than 4 hits.

AWARDS & HONORS

Hall of Fame Inductees
None

Most Valuable Players
AL: Joe DiMaggio (New York)
NL: Dolf Camilli (Brooklyn)

AL Pitching Leaders
Bob Feller (Cleveland) leads the AL with 25 wins, 260 strikeouts, and 6 shutouts. Thornton Lee (Chicago) registers the lowest ERA (2.37). Johnny Murphy (New York) picks up 15 saves.

AL Batting & Base Running Leaders
Joe DiMaggio (New York) has 125 RBI and sets an all-time major league record by hitting safely in 56 consecutive games. Ted Williams (Boston) is the first batter to hit over .400 (.406) since Bill Terry in 1930. He also slams 37 home runs and scores 135 runs. George Case (Washington) finishes first in stolen bases (33).

NL Pitching Leaders
Elmer Riddle (Cincinnati) has the lowest ERA (2.24). Brooklyn teammates Kirby Higbe and Whit Wyatt share the most wins (22). Johnny "No-Hit" Vander Meer (Cincinnati) fans 202. Lon Warneke (St. Louis) pitches the only no-hitter in the major leagues.

NL Batting & Base Running Leaders
Dolf Camilli (Brooklyn) leads the NL in HRs (34) and RBI (120). Teammate Pete Reiser bats .343. Danny Murtaugh (Philadelphia) leads the league in base-stealing with only 18.

Two of the game's greatest hitters, **Ted Williams** (l.) and **Joe DiMaggio**, celebrate Williams' 9th–inning, game–winning home run to win the 1941 All–Star game (July 8) at Tiger Stadium in Detroit. © AP

1942

REGULAR SEASON

American League
With World War II underway and all teams short on talent, the New York Yankees (103-51) repeat as AL pennant winners behind the league's best pitching staff (2.91 ERA) and best defense (142 errors, 190 double plays). Ernie Bonham (21-5), Spud Chandler (16-5) and Hank Borowy (15-4) are the mound stars. Reliever Johnny Murphy saves 11 games. Joe Gordon (.322, 103 RBI), Joe Di-Maggio (.305, 114 RBI) and Charlie Keller (.292, 26 HRs, 108 RBI) are the big guns on offense.

National League
The St. Louis Cardinals (106-48) capture their first NL flag since 1934, edging out Brooklyn by 2 games. Mort Cooper (22-7), Johnny Beazley (21-6) and Howie Krist (13-3) head up the pitching corps, which leads the NL in ERA (2.55), strikeouts (651) and shutouts (18). Only two regulars—Enos Slaughter (.318, 98 RBI) and rookie outfielder Stan Musial (.315, 72 RBI)—hit over .300.

ALL-STAR GAME & WORLD SERIES

All-Star Game (New York, NL)
The AL scores 3 runs in the 1st inning on homers by Lou Boudreau (Cleveland) and Rudy York to win, 3-1, behind strong pitching by Ernie Bonham (New York) and Al Benton (Detroit).

World Series
The St. Louis Cardinals defeat the New York Yankees, 4 games to 1, behind the strong pitching of Johnny Beazley (2 wins) and timely hitting by Walker Cooper, Jimmy Brown and the rest of the Cardinal lineup (which is out-hit by the Yankees). Phil Rizzuto (.381), Charlie Keller (2 HRs, 5 RBI) and Joe DiMaggio (.333) lead New York's offense. Red Ruffing, Yankee ace, is the first pitcher to win 7 World Series games in a career.

AWARDS & HONORS

Hall of Fame Inductee
Rogers Hornsby

Most Valuable Players
AL: Joe Gordon (New York)
NL: Mort Cooper (St. Louis)

AL Pitching Leaders
Ted Lyons (Chicago) turns in the best ERA (2.10). Tex Hughson (Boston) hurls the most wins (22) and ties Bobo Newsom (now with Washington) for most strikeouts (113). Johnny Murphy (New York) leads in saves (11) for the 2d year in a row.

AL Batting & Base Running Leaders
Boston's Ted Williams wins the AL's first Triple Crown since 1934 with a batting average of .356, 36 home runs and 137 RBI. Williams also scores the most runs (141). George Case (Washington) captures the base-stealing title (44) for the 4th straight year.

NL Pitching Leaders
Mort Cooper (St. Louis) wins the most games (22), including 10 shutouts, and compiles the leading ERA (1.78). Johnny "No- Hit" Vander Meer (Cincinnati) registers the most strikeouts (186). Hugh Casey (Brooklyn) takes over as the #1 reliever with 13 saves.

NL Batting & Base Running Leaders
Ernie Lombardi (now with Boston) wins his 2d batting title (.330). Mel Ott (New York), in his 17th year in the majors, smacks 30 homers and scores 118 runs to lead the NL. Johnny Mize (New York) has 110 RBI. Pete Reiser (Brooklyn) is the base-stealing champ (20).

1943

REGULAR SEASON

American League
The New York Yankees (98-56) continue to dominate the AL, finishing 13½ games in front of Washington. Spud Chandler (20-4), Ernie Bonham (15-8) and Johnny Murphy (12-4, 8 saves) lead the league's strongest pitching staff (2.93 ERA). Bill Dickey (.351) is the only regular to bat over .300. Nick Etten (107 RBI) and Charlie Keller (31 HRs, 86 RBI) supply the offensive punch.

National League
St. Louis (105-49) repeats as NL champions, finishing far ahead of the pack (18 games). Mort Cooper (21-8) and Max Lanier (15-7) lead a solid pitching staff that produces a 2.57 ERA, 21 shutouts, 94 complete games, and 639 strikeouts, all tops in the NL. The Cardinals' balanced hitting attack features Stan Musial (.357, 81 RBI) and Walker Cooper (.318, 81 RBI).

With a league–leading 220 hits, all–time great **Stan Musial** leads the St. Louis Cardinals to their 2d straight World Series appearance. © National Baseball Library

ALL-STAR GAME & WORLD SERIES

All-Star Game (Philadelphia, AL)
In the first All-Star game played at night, the AL comes out on top, 5-3. Bobby Doerr (Boston) slams a 3-run homer in the 2d inning to lead the way. Johnny "No-Hit" Vander Meer (Cincinnati) fans 6 consecutive AL batters.

World Series
The New York Yankees reverse the 1942 results, beating St. Louis 4 games to 1. Spud Chandler wins 2 games, allowing only 1 earned run in 18 innings. Yankee pitchers Marius Russo and Hank Borowy are also winners. Billy Johnson (.300) is the only Yankee regular to hit .300, and Marty Marion (.357) is the only Cardinal to do so.

AWARDS & HONORS

Hall of Fame Inductees
None

Most Valuable Players
AL: Spud Chandler (New York)
NL: Stan Musial (St. Louis)

AL Pitching Leaders
Spud Chandler's (New York) 1.64 ERA and 20 wins (tied with Dizzy Trout of Detroit) are the best in the majors. Allie Reynolds (Cleveland) has the most strikeouts (151). Gordon Maltzberger (Chicago) posts 14 saves.

AL Batting & Base Running Leaders
Luke Appling (Chicago) wins the AL batting title (.328). Rudy York (Detroit) pounds out the most home runs (34) and most RBI (118). George Case (Washington) steals 61 bases.

NL Pitching Leaders
Ace Adams, New York Giant relief man, appears in a record-setting 70 games. Mort Cooper (St. Louis) has the most wins (21, tied with 2 others). Cardinal teammate Howie Pollet produces the best ERA (1.75). Johnny "No-Hit" Vander Meer (Cincinnati) fans 174. Brooklyn's Les Webber saves 10 games.

NL Batting & Base Running Leaders
Stan Musial (St. Louis) wins his first batting title (.357), collects the most hits (220) and leads the NL in doubles (48) and triples (20). Bill Nicholson (Chicago) blasts 29 home runs and drives in 128 runs. Arky Vaughan (Brooklyn) steals the most bases (20).

REGULAR SEASON

American League
The St. Louis Browns (89-65) sneak past Detroit by one game to win their first pennant. Jack Kramer (17-13), Nels Potter (19-7) and George Caster (12 saves) lead the pitching staff. Shortstop Vern Stephens (.293, 20 HRs, 109 RBI) carries the offensive load.

National League
The St. Louis Cardinals (105-49) win their 3d straight NL championship, setting up the first "all-St. Louis" World Series. Mort Cooper (22-7), Ted Wilks (17-4) and Harry Brecheen (16- 5) head a good pitching staff that leads the NL in ERA (2.67), shutouts (26) and strikeouts (637). Stan Musial (.347, 94 RBI) and Ray Sanders (.295, 102 RBI) lead the offense, which smacks 100 HRs and leads the NL with a .275 batting average.

At 15, Cincinnati's **Joe Nuxhall** is the youngest player ever to appear in a major league game (June 10, 1944). © National Baseball Library

ALL-STAR GAME & WORLD SERIES

All-Star Game (Pittsburgh, NL)
The NL recovers after losing 3 straight All-Star games, winning 7-1. Phil Cavarretta (Chicago) sets an All-Star record by reaching base safely 5 times.

World Series
The St. Louis Cardinals win their 2d world championship in 3 years, upending their crosstown rivals, the Browns, 4 games to 2. Good pitching prevails on both sides (fewer than 2 earned runs per game). Mort Cooper (1-1, 16 strikeouts), Max Lanier (1-0), Harry Brecheen (1-0) and Blix Donnelly (1-0) are the big Cardinal winners. Emil Verban (.412), Walker Cooper (.318) and Stan Musial (.304) rap out 7 hits each for the Cards. Denny Galehouse (1-1, 15 strikeouts) and Jack Kramer (1-0, 12 strikeouts) star for the Browns in a losing cause. George McQuinn (.438, 5 RBI) is their batting star.

AWARDS & HONORS

Hall of Fame Inductees
None

Most Valuable Players
AL: Hal Newhouser (Detroit)
NL: Marty Marion (St. Louis)

AL Pitching Leaders
Hal Newhouser (Detroit) leads all AL pitchers with 29 wins and 187 strikeouts. The best ERA (2.12) is turned in by Tiger teammate Dizzy Trout, who also hurls 7 shutouts. Joe Nuxhall (Cincinnati) is, at 15, the youngest player ever to appear in a major league game. Three men tie for the most saves with 12.

AL Batting & Base Running Leaders
Lou Boudreau (Cleveland) leads the league in batting (.327). Snuffy Stirnweiss (New York) collects 205 hits, scores 125 runs and steals 55 bases. Teammate Nick Etten leads the home-run derby (22). Vern Stephens (St. Louis) has the most RBI (109).

NL Pitching Leaders
Bucky Walters (Cincinnati) leads the NL with the most wins (23). Ed Heusser (Cincinnati) posts a 2.38 ERA. Bill Voiselle (New York) strikes out 161, and teammate Ace Adams saves 13 games in 65 appearances. Jim Tobin (Boston) and Clyde Shoun (Cincinnati) throw no-hitters.

NL Batting & Base Running Leaders
Bill Nicholson (Chicago) blasts 33 HRs, scores 116, and drives home 122. Dixie Walker (Brooklyn) wins the batting title (.357). The top base stealer is Johnny Barrett (Pittsburgh) with 28 thefts.

REGULAR SEASON

American League
Detroit (88-65) wins its 7th AL pennant by only 1½ games over Washington. Hal Newhouser (25-9) and Dizzy Trout (18-15) head the mound staff. Rudy York (18 HRs, 87 RBI), Roy Cullenbine (18 HRs, 93 RBI) and Hank Greenberg (.311) are the Tigers' leading hitters.

National League
The Chicago Cubs (98-56) win their 10th NL pennant, beating out St. Louis by 3 games. Good team fielding and steady pitching by Claude Passeau (17-9), Hank Wyse (22-10), Hank Borowy (11-2) and Paul Derringer (16-11) are keys to Chicago's success. Phil Cavarretta (.355, 97 RBI) and Andy Pafko (.298, 110 RBI) are the Cubs' top hitters.
[Note: Jackie Robinson is signed by the Brooklyn Dodgers in 1945 and starts his career with the Dodgers' farm club in Montreal the following spring.]

ALL-STAR GAME & WORLD SERIES

All-Star Game
No game is played in 1945 because of wartime restrictions. Play resumes in 1946.

World Series
Detroit wins the Series, 4 games to 3, over the Chicago Cubs. Tiger pitching ace Hal Newhouser gives up 25 hits but strikes out 22 in winning 2 games. Dizzy Trout (1 earned run in 13⅔ innings) and Virgil Trucks are also winners for Detroit. Hank Borowy (2-2) and Claude Passeau (1-0) keep Chicago in the Series. Doc Cramer, in his 17th year, bats .379 and scores 7 runs for Detroit. Hank Greenberg (.304, 7 RBI, 7 runs scored) is another heavy contributor to the Tiger attack. Billy Nicholson (8 RBI), Stan Hack (.367) and Phil Cavarretta (.423, 5 RBI, 7 runs scored) are Chicago's big power source.

AWARDS & HONORS

Hall of Fame Inductees
Roger Bresnahan, Dan Brouthers, Fred Clarke, Jimmy Collins, Ed Delahanty, Hugh Duffy, King Kelly, Jim O'Rourke, Wilbert Robinson

Most Valuable Players
AL: Hal Newhouser (Detroit)
NL: Phil Cavarretta (Chicago)

AL Pitching Leaders
Hal Newhouser (Detroit) dominates AL pitching statistics: most wins (25), most strikeouts (212), lowest ERA (1.81), most complete games (29) and most shutouts (8). Jim Turner (New York) saves 10 games. Dick Fowler (Philadelphia) tosses the AL's only no-hitter.

AL Batting & Base Running Leaders
George Stirnweiss (New York) leads the league in hits (195), stolen bases (33) and batting average (.309; only 2 other AL players bat over .300). Vern Stephens (St. Louis) slugs 24 homers and Nick Etten (New York) drives home 111.

NL Pitching Leaders
Hank Borowy (Chicago) leads all NL pitchers with a 2.13 ERA. Red Barrett (Boston/St. Louis) collects the most wins (23). Preacher Roe (Pittsburgh) fans 148. Ace Adams (New York) and Andy Karl (Philadelphia) pick up 15 saves each.

NL Batting & Base Running Leaders
Phil Cavarretta (Chicago) has the NL's best batting average (.355). Tommy Holmes (Boston) pounds out 28 home runs. Red Schoendienst (St. Louis) leads in steals with 26.

1946

REGULAR SEASON

American League
The Boston Red Sox (104-50) combine good hitting (.271 team average) and fielding (only 139 errors) to capture the pennant by 12 games over 1945 champion Detroit. Ted Williams (.342, 38 HRs, 123 RBI), Rudy York (119 RBI) and Bobby Doerr (116 RBI) are Boston's big-run producers. Boo Ferriss (25-6), Tex Hughson (20-11) and Mickey Harris (17-9) head up the pitching corps.

National League
St. Louis and Brooklyn end the season in a tie (96-58). The Cardinals win the pennant in a playoff, 2 games to 0, over the Dodgers. Howie Pollet (21-10) leads the pitching staff, which is #1 in the NL in ERA (3.01) and shutouts (18). Enos Slaughter (.300, 18 HRs, 130 RBI) and Stan Musial (.365, 16 HRs, 103 RBI) pace the Cardinal offense.

ALL-STAR GAME & WORLD SERIES

All-Star Game (Boston, AL)
Ted Williams (Boston) leads the hit-fest with a record-setting 5 RBI on 4 hits, including 2 homers, as the AL swamps the NL, 12-0.

World Series
St. Louis defeats Boston, 4 games to 3, in a close Series. Harry Brecheen is the Cardinal pitching hero, winning 3 games (one in relief) giving up only 1 earned run over 20 innings. Harry Walker (.412, 6 RBI), Enos Slaughter (.320, 5 runs scored) and Whitey Kurowski (.296, 5 runs scored) are the chief run producers for St. Louis. Bobby Doerr (.409) and Rudy York (2 HRs, 5 RBI) lead the Red Sox attack. Boston ace Boo Ferriss pitches the 50th shutout in World Series history (game 3). Slaughter scores the winning run in game 7 when Johnny Pesky, Boston's shortstop, fails to throw home in time.

AWARDS & HONORS

Hall of Fame Inductees
Jesse Burkett, Frank Chance, Jack Chesbro, Johnny Evers, Buck Ewing, Clark Griffith, Tommy McCarthy, Joe "Iron Man" McGinnity, Eddie Plank, Joe Tinker, Rube Waddell, Ed Walsh

Most Valuable Players
AL: Ted Williams (Boston)
NL: Stan Musial (St. Louis)

AL Pitching Leaders
Hal Newhouser (Detroit) and Bob Feller (Cleveland) have the most wins (26). Newhouser has the best ERA (1.94) while Feller strikes out 348 (major league record) and hurls 36 complete games, including 10 shutouts. He also tosses the only no-hitter (his career 2d) in the AL during 1946.

AL Batting & Base Running Leaders
Mickey Vernon (Washington) wins the batting title (.353). Hank Greenberg (Detroit) clouts 44 HRs and has 127 RBI. Ted Williams (Boston) draws 156 walks, scores 142 runs, and is second in batting average, home runs and RBI. George Case returns as the stolen-base leader (28).

NL Pitching Leaders
Howie Pollet (St. Louis) wins 21 games with a 2.10 ERA to lead the league. Johnny Schmitz (Chicago) fans 135. Ken Raffensberger (Philadelphia) notches 6 saves. Brooklyn's Ed Head twirls a no-hitter.

NL Batting & Base Running Leaders
Stan Musial (St. Louis) wins his 2d batting title (.365). Ralph Kiner (Pittsburgh) smacks 23 HRs, and Enos Slaughter (St. Louis) drives in 130 runs. Pete Reiser (Brooklyn) is the #1 base stealer (34).

In the 7th game of the 1946 World Series (October 15), **Enos Slaughter** of St. Louis races home from first on a single for the winning run against Boston. © AP

1947

REGULAR SEASON

American League
The New York Yankees (97-57) win the AL flag by 12 games over Detroit. Allie Reynolds (19-8), Spec Shea (14-5), Spud Chandler (9-5, 2.46 ERA) and Joe Page (17 saves) set the pace for a pitching staff that has the lowest ERA (3.39) and the most strikeouts (691) in the league. Joe DiMaggio (.315, 20 HRs, 97 RBI), Tommy Henrich (.287, 16 HRs, 98 RBI) and Billy Johnson (.285, 95 RBI) supply the firepower.

National League
Jackie Robinson (Brooklyn) is the first black man to play in the major leagues. He helps the Brooklyn Dodgers (94-60) nose out the St. Louis Cardinals by 5 games to win the pennant. Ralph Branca (21-12), Joe Hatten (17-8) and reliever Hugh Casey (10-4, 18 saves) star on the mound. Robinson (.297), Dixie Walker (.306, 94 RBI), Carl Furillo (.295, 88 RBI) and Pee Wee Reese (.284, 73 RBI) excel on the field as well as at the plate.

ALL-STAR GAME & WORLD SERIES

All-Star Game (Chicago, NL)
The AL squeaks by the NL, 2-1, on a throwing error by Boston Braves' pitcher Johnny Sain.

World Series
The New York Yankees defeat Brooklyn as the World Series goes the full 7 games for the 3d year in a row. Rookie pitcher Spec Shea wins 2 games for New York. Reliever Joe Page saves one game and wins another. Johnny Lindell (.500, 7 RBI), Tommy Henrich (.333, 5 RBI) and Billy Johnson (8 runs scored) star at bat for the Yankees. Yogi Berra also hits the first pinch-hit homer in World Series history. Brooklyn's Hugh Casey (2-0) allows but 1 earned run in 10 1/3 innings in a losing cause.

AWARDS & HONORS

Hall of Fame Inductees
Mickey Cochrane, Frankie Frisch, Lefty Grove, Carl Hubbell

Most Valuable Players
AL: Joe DiMaggio (New York)
NL: Bob Elliott (Boston)

Rookie of the Year
Jackie Robinson (Brooklyn)

AL Pitching Leaders
Spud Chandler's (New York) ERA of 2.46 is the best in the AL. Bob Feller (Cleveland) registers 20 wins and 196 strikeouts. Ed Klieman (Cleveland) ties Joe Page (New York) for the most saves (17). Don Black (Cleveland) and Bill McCahan (Philadelphia) both throw no-hitters.

AL Batting & Base Running Leaders
Ted Williams (Boston) leads the way for AL hitters in batting average (.343), HRs (32) and RBI (114) to win the Triple Crown. Bob Dillinger (St. Louis) is #1 in stolen bases (34).

NL Pitching Leaders
Ewell Blackwell (Cincinnati) wins 22 games, throws the only NL no-hitter of the season, and strikes out 193. Warren Spahn (Boston) posts a 2.33 ERA. Hugh Casey saves 18 games for Brooklyn.

NL Batting & Base Running Leaders
Johnny Mize (New York) has a league-high 138 RBI and ties Pittsburgh's Ralph Kiner with 51 home runs. Harry "The Hat" Walker (St. Louis) takes the batting crown (.363). Jackie Robinson (Brooklyn's Rookie of the Year) leads in stolen bases (29).

1948

REGULAR SEASON

American League
Though Cleveland and Boston finish the season tied for first place (96-58), the Indians win the pennant in a 1-game playoff. Bob Lemon (20-14), Bob Feller (19-15) and Gene Bearden (20-7) head up a strong pitching staff (3.22 ERA, 30 saves, 26 shutouts). Joe Gordon (.280, 32 HRs, 124 RBI), player/manager Lou Boudreau (.355, 106 RBI) and Ken Keltner (.297, 31 HRs, 119 RBI) provide the offensive punch.

National League
Boston (91-62) wins its first pennant since 1914, beating St. Louis by 6½ games. Johnny Sain (24-15), Vern Bickford (11- 5) and Warren Spahn (15-2) spark the pitching staff, which has the lowest ERA (3.38) in the NL. Bob Elliott (.283, 23 HRs, 100 RBI) and Jeff Heath (.319, 20 HRs, 76 RBI) supply most of the Braves' offense.

ALL-STAR GAME & WORLD SERIES

All-Star Game (St. Louis, AL)
The AL defeats the NL, 5-2, helped by a 2-run single stroked by Yankee pitcher Vic Raschi.

World Series
Cleveland defeats the Boston Braves in a low-scoring Series, 4 games to 2, behind excellent pitching and timely hitting. Although Cleveland ace Bob Feller loses 2 games, Bob Lemon comes through with 2 wins and a 1.65 ERA. Steve Gromek and Gene Bearden also post wins for Cleveland (Bearden gets credit for a save in the game 6 clincher as well).

AWARDS & HONORS

Hall of Fame Inductees
Herb Pennock, Pie Traynor

Most Valuable Players
AL: Lou Boudreau (Cleveland)
NL: Stan Musial (St. Louis)

Rookie of the Year
Alvin Dark (Boston, NL)

AL Pitching Leaders
Hal Newhouser (Detroit) has the most wins (21) for the 3d time in 4 years, and Bob Feller (Cleveland) leads in strikeouts (164) for the 3d straight year. Gene Bearden (Cleveland) has the best ERA (2.43) and teammate Bob Lemon tosses 10 shutouts and hurls a no-hitter. Russ Christopher, another Cleveland pitcher, earns the most saves (17).

AL Batting & Base Running Leaders
Joe DiMaggio (New York) leads the AL in homers (39) and RBI (155). Ted Williams (Boston) wins his 4th batting title (.369). Bob Dillinger (St. Louis) takes the base-stealing crown (28).

NL Pitching Leaders
Johnny Sain (Boston) picks up the most wins (24). Harry Brecheen (St. Louis) leads in strikeouts (149), ERA (2.24) and shutouts (7). Harry Gumbert (Cincinnati) saves 17 games. Rex Barney (Brooklyn) fashions a no-hitter against New York.

NL Batting & Base Running Leaders
Stan Musial (St. Louis) wins his 3d batting title (.376). He also leads the NL in RBI (131), runs scored (135) and hits (230). Ralph Kiner (Pittsburgh) and Johnny Mize (New York) again tie for the most home runs (40). Richie Ashburn (Philadelphia) takes over as stolen-base king (32).

The classic swing of Hall of Famer **Joe DiMaggio.** Joltin' Joe played in 10 World Series for the New York Yankees. © Wide World

1949

REGULAR SEASON

American League
The New York Yankees (97-57), led by their new manager, Casey Stengel, win their 16th pennant, edging out Boston by one game. Yankee mound leaders are Vic Raschi (21-10), Allie Reynolds (17-6), Joe Page (13-8, 27 saves) and Ed Lopat (15-10). Tommy Henrich (.287, 2 HRs, 85 RBI) and Yogi Berra (20 HRs, 91 RBI) pace the offense.

National League
The Brooklyn Dodgers (97-57) capture their 2d pennant in 3 years, squeezing past St. Louis by one game. Rookie pitcher Don Newcombe (17-8) and veterans Preacher Roe (15-6) and Ralph Branca (13-5) lead the pitching staff, which registers the most strikeouts (743) and shutouts (15) in the league. The offense is led by Duke Snider (.292, 23 HRs, 92 RBI), Carl Furillo (.322, 106 RBI), Jackie Robinson (.342, 124 RBI) and Gil Hodges (.285, 23 HRs, 115 RBI).

ALL-STAR GAME & WORLD SERIES

All-Star Game (Brooklyn, NL)
The AL defeats the NL in a slugfest, 11-7. Jackie Robinson, Roy Campanella and Don Newcombe (all of Brooklyn) and Larry Doby (Cleveland) become the first black players in an All-Star game.

World Series
The New York Yankees defeat Brooklyn for the 3d time in the last 9 Series, 4 games to 1, for their 12th world championship. Superior pitching (2.80 ERA, 38 strikeouts) is the key factor. Vic Raschi, Allie Reynolds, Joe Page and Ed Lopat win one game each. Bobby Brown (.500) and Gene Woodling (.400) star at bat for New York. Preacher Roe hurls a 6-hit shutout in game 2 for Brooklyn's only win. Pee Wee Reese (.316) is the only Dodger to bat over .300.

AWARDS & HONORS

Hall of Fame Inductees
Charlie Gehringer, Mordecai Brown, Kid Nichols

Most Valuable Players
AL: Ted Williams (Boston)
NL: Jackie Robinson (Brooklyn)

Rookies of the Year
AL: Roy Sievers (St. Louis)
NL: Don Newcombe (Brooklyn)

AL Pitching Leaders
Joe Page saves 27 games for New York. Mel Parnell (Boston) wins 25 games and records the best ERA (2.77). Virgil Trucks (Detroit) strikes out 153.

AL Batting & Base Running Leaders
Ted Williams (Boston) and teammate Vern Stephens tie for the most RBI (159). Williams also blasts 43 homers, walks 162 times, and loses the batting championship by a fraction of one-percent to George Kell of Detroit (.343). Bob Dillinger (St. Louis) is the base-stealing champ (20) for the 3d year in a row.

NL Pitching Leaders
Dave Koslo (New York) leads the NL with a 2.50 ERA. Warren Spahn (Boston) has the most wins (21), most strikeouts (151) and most complete games (25).

NL Batting & Base Running Leaders
Ralph Kiner (Pittsburgh) hits the most home runs (54) for the 4th year in a row. He also leads in RBI (127). Jackie Robinson wins the batting title (.342) and steals the most bases (37).

1950

REGULAR SEASON

American League
The New York Yankees (98-67) continue their dominance in the AL, finishing the season 3 games ahead of Detroit and 4 in front of Boston. New York's pitching staff is solid with Vic Raschi (21-8), Ed Lopat (18-8), Allie Reynolds (16-12) and Tommy Byrne (15-9) carrying the load. At the plate, Joe DiMaggio (.301, 32 HRs, 122 RBI), Yogi Berra (.322, 28 HRs, 124 RBI) and Johnny Mize (25 HRs) supply the power.

National League
Philadelphia's "Whiz Kids" (91-63) surprise the NL by finishing ahead of Brooklyn (2 games) and New York (5 games). Robin Roberts (20-11), Curt Simmons (17-8) and reliever Jim Konstanty (16-7, 22 saves) are the pitching heroes on a staff that leads the NL with a 3.50 ERA and 27 saves. Del Ennis (.311, 31 HRs, 126 RBI) has a big year at the plate.

ALL-STAR GAME & WORLD SERIES

All-Star Game (Chicago, AL)
In the longest game in All-Star history (14 innings), the NL wins, 4-3, on a solo home run by Red Schoendienst. Ted Williams (Boston) breaks his elbow making a sensational catch and misses the rest of the season.

World Series
The New York Yankees sweep Philadelphia's "Whiz Kids," 4 games to 0. Pitchers Vic Raschi, Eddie Lopat, Allie Reynolds and rookie Whitey Ford have a combined 0.73 ERA and walk only 7 men in 4 games. Gene Woodling (.429) is the leading Yankee at bat. Philadelphia's pitching staff allows 2.27 ERA, normally good enough to win. Granny Hamner (.429) is the only Philly regular to bat over .300 in the Series.

AWARDS & HONORS

Hall of Fame Inductees
None

Most Valuable Players
AL: Phil Rizzuto (New York)
NL: Jim Konstanty (Philadelphia)

Rookies of the Year:
AL: Walt Dropo (Boston)
NL: Sam Jethroe (Boston)

AL Pitching Leaders
Bob Lemon (Cleveland) wins 23 games and strikes out 170 to lead the AL. Early Wynn (Cleveland) posts the best ERA (3.20). Mickey Harris (Washington) has the most saves (15).

AL Batting & Base Running Leaders
Billy Goodman (Boston) wins the AL batting title (.354). With 37 home runs, Cleveland's Al Rosen leads the league and sets a new record for homers by a rookie. Boston teammates Walt Dropo and Vern Stephens tie for most RBI (144). Another Boston player, Dom Di-Maggio (Joe's brother) steals the most bases (15).

NL Pitching Leaders
Jim Konstanty (Philadelphia) racks up 22 saves. Warren Spahn (Boston) picks up 22 wins and fans 191. Jim Hearn (New York/St. Louis) has the best ERA (2.49). Vern Bickford (Boston) throws the only no-hitter in the major leagues during 1950.

NL Batting & Base Running Leaders
Stan Musial (St. Louis) and Ralph Kiner (Pittsburgh) again lead all NL hitters. Kiner hits 47 HRs and Musial takes the batting title (.346). Duke Snider (Brooklyn) collects the most hits (199). Del Ennis (Philadelphia) drives in 126 runs. Sam Jethroe (Boston) leads in stolen bases (35).

1951

REGULAR SEASON

American League
The New York Yankees (98-56) win their 3d pennant in a row, beating out Cleveland by 5 games. Vic Raschi (21-10), Allie Reynolds (17-8) and Eddie Lopat (21-9) lead the AL's best pitching staff (664 strikeouts, 24 shutouts). Gil McDougald (.306) is the only Yankee to bat over .300, and no player has more than 88 RBI. Future Hall of Famer Joe DiMaggio retires at the end of the season.

National League
New York and Brooklyn end the season tied for 1st place (96-58). The Giants capture the flag in a dramatic playoff, 2 games to 1, as Bobby Thomson's "shot heard round the world" wins it all for New York. Sal Maglie (23-6) and Larry Jansen (23-11) lead the NL's best pitching staff (3.48 ERA). Monte Irvin (.312, 24 HRs, 121 RBI) and Thomson (.293, 32 HRs, 101 RBI) are the offensive stars.

ALL-STAR GAME & WORLD SERIES

All-Star Game (Detroit, AL)
The NL defeats the AL, 8-3, marking the first time it has won back-to-back All-Star games. An All-Star game record is set when 6 homers are hit (4 by the NL, 2 by the AL).

World Series
In still another New York "Subway Series," the Yankees retain their world championship (#14), defeating the Giants, 4 games to 2. Ed Lopat stars on the mound for the Yankees, winning 2 games and allowing only 1 run in 18 innings. Gil McDougald leads in RBI (7, including a grand slam in game 5) and Phil Rizzuto collects the most hits (8). Alvin Dark (.417) and Monte Irvin (.458) are the leading Giant batsmen. Hank Bauer's bases loaded triple in game 6 is the clincher for the American Leaguers.

AWARDS & HONORS

Hall of Fame Inductees
Jimmy Foxx, Mel Ott

Most Valuable Players
AL: Yogi Berra (New York)
NL: Roy Campanella (Brooklyn)

Rookies of the Year
AL: Gil McDougald (New York)
NL: Willie Mays (New York)

AL Pitching Leaders
Bob Feller (Cleveland) turns in the most wins (22). Vic Raschi (New York) strikes out 164, and Saul Rogovin (Chicago/Detroit) posts the best ERA (2.78). Ellis Kinder (Boston) has the most saves. Bob Feller also hurls his 3d career no-hitter, and Allie Reynolds (New York) tosses 2 no-hit, no-run games (the 1st AL pitcher to do so in one season).

AL Batting & Base Running Leaders
Ferris Fain (Philadelphia) wins the batting crown (.344) and teammate Gus Zernial leads in RBI (129) and home runs (33). Minnie Minoso (Chicago) has the most steals (31).

NL Pitching Leaders
Sal Maglie and Larry Jansen, New York Giant teammates, share the most-wins title (23). Don Newcombe (Brooklyn) and Warren Spahn (Boston) tie for the most strikeouts (164). Chet Nichols (Boston) has the best ERA (2.88). Ted Wilks (Pittsburgh/St. Louis) collects the most saves (13) and Pittsburgh's Cliff Chambers throw the only NL no-hitter.

NL Batting & Base Running Leaders
Ralph Kiner (Pittsburgh) leads the NL in home runs (42) and Monte Irvin (New York) knocks in 121 runs. Stan Musial (St. Louis) wins his 4th batting title (.355). Sam Jethroe (Boston) is the top base stealer (35) for the 2d year in a row.

The New York Giants mob teammate **Bobby Thomson** following his 3–run homer off Brooklyn's Ralph Branca—the "shot heard 'round the world" (October 3)—to win the 1951 NL pennant. © AP

1952

REGULAR SEASON

American League
New York (95-59) sneaks past Cleveland by 2 games to capture its 4th straight pennant. Allie Reynolds (20-8, 2.06 ERA) and Vic Raschi (16-6) lead the pitching staff (3.14 ERA). Rookie outfielder Mickey Mantle replaces Joe DiMaggio in the lineup and bats .311 with 23 HRs and 87 RBI. Yogi Berra (30 HRs, 98 RBI) is the team's leading run producer.

National League
The Brooklyn Dodgers (96-57) nail down the NL pennant, beating out the New York Giants by 4½ games. Rookie relief pitcher Joe Black (15-4) saves 15 games. Carl Erskine (14-6), Preacher Roe (11-2) and Billy Loes (13-8) round out a well-balanced mound corps. Gil Hodges (32 HRs, 102 RBI), Roy Campanella (22 HRs, 97 RBI) and Duke Snider (21 HRs, 92 RBI) lead the club in hitting.

ALL-STAR GAME & WORLD SERIES

All-Star Game (Philadelphia, NL)
The NL defeats the AL, 3-2, for its 3d straight win. The game is called off at the end of 5 innings because of rain. Home runs by Brooklyn's Jackie Robinson and Hank Sauer (Chicago) account for all NL runs.

World Series
In a dramatic 7-game Series, the New York Yankees defeat Brooklyn for the 4th time in Series play. Mickey Mantle (.345), Gene Woodling (.348) and Johnny Mize (.400, 3 HRs, 6 RBI) lead the offense. Allie Reynolds (2-1) and Vic Raschi (2-0) allow a combined 7 earned runs in 37⅓ innings. Joe Black, Carl Erskine and Preacher Roe win 1 game apiece for the Dodgers. Pee Wee Reese (.345) and Duke Snider (.345, 4 HRs, 8 RBI) lead Brooklyn's attack. In the 7th and deciding game, Bob Kuzava, the 4th Yankee pitcher, retires the last 8 Dodgers in order to save the game and Series for New York.

AWARDS & HONORS

Hall of Fame Inductees
Harry Heilmann, Paul Waner

Most Valuable Players
AL: Bobby Schantz (Philadelphia)
NL: Hank Sauer (Chicago)

Rookies of the Year
AL: Harry Byrd (Philadelphia)
NL: Joe Black (Brooklyn)

AL Pitching Leaders
Bobby Schantz (Philadelphia) leads the AL with 24 wins. Allie Reynolds (New York) fans 160 and has the lowest ERA (2.06). Harry Dorish (Chicago) is the top reliever (11 saves). Virgil Trucks (Detroit) becomes the 2d AL pitcher to throw 2 no-hitters in one season.

AL Batting & Base Running Leaders
Larry Doby (Cleveland) leads the HR parade (32) and teammate Al Rosen tops the league with 105 RBI. Ferris Fain (Philadelphia) repeats as batting champion (.327). Minnie Minoso (Chicago) retains his stolen-base title (22).

NL Pitching Leaders
Hoyt Wilhelm, New York's relief ace, boasts the NL's best ERA (2.43). Robin Roberts (Philadelphia) wins 28 games and Warren Spahn strikes out 183. Al Brazle (St. Louis) has the most saves (16) and Carl Erskine (Brooklyn) pitches the NL's only no-hitter of the season.

NL Batting & Base Running Leaders
Ralph Kiner (Pittsburgh) and Hank Sauer (Chicago) tie for the most HRs (37) but Sauer takes RBI honors with 121. Stan Musial (St. Louis) repeats as batting champion (.336). He also has the most hits (194) and doubles (42). Pee Wee Reese (Brooklyn) is the new stolen-base leader (30).

1953

REGULAR SEASON

American League
The New York Yankees (99-52) roll on to their 5th straight pennant, finishing 8½ games ahead of Cleveland. Whitey Ford (18-6), Johnny Sain (14-7), Vic Raschi (13-6) and Eddie Lopat (16-4, 2.42 ERA) lead the AL's #1 pitching staff (3.20 ERA, 39 saves). Yogi Berra (.296, 27 HRs, 108 RBI) and Mickey Mantle (.295, 21 HRs, 92 RBI) pace the Yankee attack.

National League
Brooklyn (105-49) repeats as NL champions, finishing far ahead of the Milwaukee Braves (who had moved from Boston during the off season). Carl Erskine (20-6), Russ Meyer (15-5), Preacher Roe (11-3), Billy Loes (14-8) and reliever Clem Labine (11-6) are the top pitchers. Roy Campanella (.312, 41 HRs, 142 RBI), Gil Hodges (.302, 31 HRs, 122 RBI), Carl Furillo (.344, 21 HRs, 92 RBI) and Duke Snider (.336, 42 HRs, 126 RBI) lead the NL's most powerful offense.

ALL-STAR GAME & WORLD SERIES

All-Star Game (Cincinnati, NL)
The NL takes its 4th All-Star game in a row, 5-1. Enos Slaughter (St. Louis) stars at bat and in the field for the winners.

World Series
Brooklyn loses the Series to New York for the 2d year in a row and the 5th time in the last 12 years. Billy Martin is the hitting star for New York (12 hits in 24 at bats and 8 RBI). Yogi Berra (.429) and Mickey Mantle (2 HRs, 7 RBI) are also heavy contributors to the Yankee attack. Eddie Lopat, Allie Reynolds, Johnny Sain and Jim McDonald all get credit for a Series win. Brooklyn collects 8 more hits than New York but cannot stop the Yankees' 5th straight world championship (a new record).

AWARDS & HONORS

Hall of Fame Inductees
Dizzy Dean, Al Simmons, Bobby Wallace

Most Valuable Players
AL: Al Rosen (Cleveland)
NL: Roy Campanella (Brooklyn)

Rookies of the Year
AL: Harvey Kuenn (Detroit)
NL: Junior Gilliam (Brooklyn)

AL Pitching Leaders
Ed Lopat (New York) has the best ERA (2.42) and Bob Porterfield (Washington) has the most wins (22). Billy Pierce (Chicago) leads in strikeouts (186) and shutouts (9). Reliever Ellis Kinder (Boston) is credited with 27 saves. Bob Holloman (St. Louis) hurls a no-hitter in his first major league appearance.

AL Batting & Base Running Leaders
Al Rosen (Cleveland) slams 43 home runs and drives in 143 to lead the league. Mickey Vernon (Washington) takes the batting title (.337). Minnie Minoso (Chicago) regains the stolen-base crown (25).

NL Pitching Leaders
Warren Spahn (Milwaukee) and Robin Roberts (Philadelphia) tie for the most wins (23). Spahn's ERA (2.10) is tops and Roberts is #1 in strikeouts (198) and complete games (33). Al Brazle (St. Louis) leads in saves (18).

NL Batting & Base Running Leaders
Eddie Matthews (Milwaukee), in only his 2d year, slams 47 homers. Roy Campanella (Brooklyn) tops the NL in RBI (142), while teammate Carl Furillo wins the batting crown (.344). Bill Bruton (Milawukee) takes over as the #1 base stealer (26).

REGULAR SEASON

American League
The Cleveland Indians win 111 games (most in the modern era) and break the Yankees' string of 5 pennants, finishing 8 games in front of New York. Early Wynn (23-11), Bob Lemon (23-7), Mike Garcia (19- 8), Bob Feller (13-3) and reliever Ray Narleski (13 saves) lead the league's top mound corps (2.78 ERA). Larry Doby (32 HRs, 126 RBI), Bobby Avila (.341) and Al Rosen (.300, 24 HRs, 102 RBI) are the team's leading hitters.

National League
The New York Giants (97-57), led by manager Leo Durocher, win the pennant by 5 games over Brooklyn. Johnny Antonelli (21-7, 2.30 ERA), Ruben Gomez (17-9, 2.88 ERA), Sal Maglie (14-6) and reliever Hoyt Wilhelm (12-4, 7 saves, 2.10 ERA) anchor a strong pitching staff (3.09 ERA). Willie Mays (.345, 41 HRs, 110 RBI) and Hank Thompson (26 HRs, 86 RBI) lead the team in hitting.

New York Giant center fielder **Willie Mays** makes "the catch," hauling in Vic Wertz's 440–foot drive in the 8th inning of the opening game of the 1954 World Series vs. the Cleveland Indians (September 29). © AP

ALL-STAR GAME & WORLD SERIES

All-Star Game (Cleveland, AL)
After losing 5 straight games, the AL comes out on top, 11-9, in a 31-hit slug-fest, highlighted by 6 homers (2 by Cleveland's Al Rosen). It is the highest-scoring game in All-Star history.

World Series
The New York Giants sweep Cleveland, 4 games to 0, as its pitching staff twirls a combined 1.46 ERA. Johnny Antonelli, Ruben Gomez, Don Liddle and Marv Grissom (in relief) win 1 game each. Dusty Rhodes stars in a pinch-hitting role for the Giants with 7 RBI. Don Mueller (.389), Alvin Dark (.412) and Hank Thompson (.364) provide more punch to the Giant offense (which fails to hit a home run). Vic Wertz (.500) is the only Cleveland batter to solve the Giants' pitching as New York takes its 4th world championship. Willie Mays of the Giants makes a sensational catch in game 1 to rob Wertz of at least a triple (see photo).

AWARDS & HONORS

Hall of Fame Inductees
Bill Dickey, Rabbit Maranville, Bill Terry

Most Valuable Players
AL: Yogi Berra (New York)
NL: Willie Mays (New York)

Rookies of the Year
AL: Bob Grim (New York)
NL: Wally Moon (St. Louis)

AL Pitching Leaders
Mike Garcia (Cleveland) registers a 2.64 ERA to lead the AL. His Indian teammates Bob Lemon and Early Wynn share the most wins (23). Wynn ties Bob Turley (New York) for most strikeouts (185). Johnny Sain (New York) has the most saves (22).

AL Batting & Base Running Leaders
Larry Doby (Cleveland) leads the AL in home runs (32) and RBI (126). Bobby Avila (Cleveland) takes the batting title (.341). Jackie Jensen (Boston) steals the most bases (22).

NL Pitching Leaders
Johnny Antonelli's (New York) 6 shutouts and 2.30 ERA are best in the NL. Robin Roberts (Philadelphia) has the most wins (23), most strikeouts (185) and most complete games (29). Jim Hughes (Brooklyn) is the top NL relief ace with 29 saves. Jim Wilson (Milwaukee) tosses the only no-hitter in the major leagues for the 1954 season.

NL Batting & Base Running Leaders
Ted Kluszewski (Cincinnati) hits 49 homers and drives in 141 to lead all NL sluggers. Willie Mays (New York) wins his first (and only) batting title (.345). Bill Bruton (Milwaukee) repeats as the stolen-base champ (34).

REGULAR SEASON

American League

The New York Yankees (96-58) capture the AL pennant by 3 games over Cleveland behind the strong pitching of Whitey Ford (18-7, 2.63 ERA), Bob Turley (17-13) and Tommy Byrne (16-5). Yogi Berra (27 HRs, 108 RBI) and Mickey Mantle (.306, 37 HRs, 99 RBI) are the big run producers. [Note: The Philadelphia A's franchise is transferred to Kansas City, Missouri.]

National League

The Brooklyn Dodgers (98-55) run away with the NL pennant by 13½ games over Milwaukee. Duke Snider (.309, 42 HRs, 136 RBI), Gil Hodges (.289, 27 HRs, 102 RBI), Roy Campanella (.318, 32 HRs, 107 RBI) and Carl Furillo (.314, 26 HRs, 95 RBI) lead a potent offense that leads the NL in batting (.271) and home runs (201). Don Newcombe (20-5), Clem Labine (13-5), Billy Loes (10-4) and Don Bessent (8-1) head the #1 pitching staff (3.68 ERA, 37 saves, 773 strikeouts).

ALL-STAR GAME & WORLD SERIES

All-Star Game (Milwaukee, NL)

The NL defeats the AL, 6-5, in a 12-inning thriller. Gene Conley (Milwaukee) strikes out the side in the 12th inning and Stan Musial (St. Louis) wins it with a homer. Mickey Mantle (New York) blasts a 3-run homer in the 1st inning to give the AL a lead it could not hold.

World Series

The Brooklyn Dodgers win their only World Series, defeating their nemesis, the New York Yankees (who had won 6 world championships without a loss until 1955), 4 games to 3. Johnny Podres (2-0, 1.00 ERA) is the mound hero for the Dodgers. Clem Labine and Roger Craig are also winners. Duke Snider (.320, 4 HRs, 7 RBI) leads the offense, which slams 9 home runs and 8 doubles. Whitey Ford (2-0) stars for the Yankees in a losing cause. Yogi Berra (.417) and Billy Martin (.320) are the top hitters for New York. The Yankees commit only 2 errors in the 7-game Series.

AWARDS & HONORS

Hall of Fame Inductees

Joe DiMaggio, Gabby Hartnett, Frank Baker, Ted Lyons, Ray Schalk, Dazzy Vance.

Most Valuable Players

AL: Yogi Berra (New York)
NL: Roy Campanella (Broooklyn)

Rookies of the Year

AL: Herb Score (Cleveland)
NL: Bill Virdon (St. Louis)

AL Pitching Leaders

Whitey Ford (New York) shares the most wins (18) with Bob Lemon (Cleveland) and Frank Sullivan (Boston). Billy Pierce (Chicago) has the best ERA (1.97). Ray Narleski (Cleveland) saves 19 games. Herb Score's (Cleveland) 245 strikeouts lead the (AL) and set a new record for strikeouts by a rookie.

AL Batting & Base Running Leaders

Mickey Mantle (New York) cranks out 37 homers. Ray Boone (Detroit) and Jackie Jensen (Boston) each drive in 116 to lead the AL. Al Kaline (Detroit), the only player to get 200 or more hits, wins the batting crown (.340). Jim Rivera (Chicago) leads in stolen bases (25).

NL Pitching Leaders

Sam Jones (Chicago) racks up 198 strikeouts and hurls the only no-hitter in the NL in 1955. Robin Roberts (Philadelphia) wins 23 games. Bob Friend (Pittsburgh) has the lowest ERA (2.83). Jack Meyer (Philadelphia) leads in saves with 16.

NL Batting & Base Running Leaders

Willie Mays (New York) leads in homers (51). Duke Snider's (Brooklyn) 136 RBI are tops in the league. Richie Ashburn (Philadelphia) is the batting champ (.338). Bill Bruton (Milwaukee) leads in stolen bases (25) for the 3d straight year.

Brooklyn Dodger star **Jackie Robinson** steals home during the opening game of the 1955 World Series vs. the New York Yankees (September 28). Pinch–hitter **Frank Kellert** is at bat; **Yogi Berra** is the catcher. © UPI

1956

REGULAR SEASON

American League
The New York Yankees (97-57) retain the AL championship, finishing 9 games in front of Cleveland. Whitey Ford (19-6), Johnny Kucks (18-9), Don Larsen (11-5) and Tom Sturdivant (16-8) are the mound stars. Mickey Mantle (.353, 52 HRs, 130 RBI) enjoys his best year at the plate. Moose Skowron (.308, 23 HRs, 90 RBI) and Yogi Berra (.298, 30 HRs, 105 RBI) are also heavy contributors to the Yankee attack.

National League
The Brooklyn Dodgers (93-61) wind up in front for the 2d year in a row, edging out Milwaukee by one game. Don Newcombe (27-7), Sal Maglie (13-5) and Clem Labine (19 saves) lead the mound corps. Duke Snider (.292, 43 HRs, 101 RBI) is the big run producer. Brooklyn's defense leads the league with only 111 errors.

New York Yankee pitcher **Don Larsen** tosses a perfect game in the 5th game of the 1956 World Series (October 8) to beat the Brooklyn Dodgers 2–0. It is the only no–hitter in Series' history. © UPI

ALL-STAR GAME & WORLD SERIES

All-Star Game (Washington, AL)
Ken Boyer (St. Louis) leads the NL with his bat and his glove, defeating the AL 7-3. Ted Williams (Boston) and Mickey Mantle (New York) hit back-to-back homers in the 6th inning for all 3 AL runs. Willie Mays (New York) and Stan Musial (St. Louis) connect for the NL.

World Series
The New York Yankees recapture the world championship, defeating the Brooklyn Dodgers in a re-match, 4 games to 3. Don Larsen startles the baseball world by pitching a perfect game (27 batters retired in order), the first no-hitter in World Series history. Whitey Ford, Johnny Kucks and Tom Sturdivant are the other Yankee winners. Yogi Berra (.360, 3 HRs, 10 RBI) is the hitting star for New York. Clem Labine hurls 10 shutout innings in game 6 to even the Series for Brooklyn. Gil Hodges (8 RBI) leads the Dodger offense.

AWARDS & HONORS

Hall of Fame Inductees
Joe Cronin, Hank Greenberg

Most Valuable Players
AL: Mickey Mantle (New York)
NL: Don Newcombe (Brooklyn)

Rookies of the Year
AL: Luis Aparicio (Chicago)
NL: Frank Robinson (Cincinnati)

Cy Young Award Winner
Don Newcombe (Brooklyn, NL)

AL Pitching Leaders
Frank Lary (Detroit) picks up the most wins (21). Herb Score (Cleveland) strikes out 265 to lead the majors. Whitey Ford's (New York) ERA (2.47) is tops in the AL. George Zuverink (Baltimore) is the top reliever (16 saves).

AL Batting & Base Running Leaders
Mickey Mantle (New York) leads the league in batting (.353), home runs (52) and RBI (130) to become the first Triple Crown winner in the major leagues since Ted Williams in 1947. Rookie Luis Aparicio (Chicago) is the base-stealing champ (21).

NL Pitching Leaders
Don Newcombe (Brooklyn) wins 27 games. Sam Jones (Chicago) leads in strikeouts (176) and Lew Burdette (Milwaukee) has the best ERA (2.70). Clem Labine (Brooklyn) notches the most saves (19), while teammates Carl Erskine and Sal Maglie both pitch no-hitters.

NL Batting & Base Running Leaders
Duke Snider (Brooklyn) leads the home-run parade with 43. Hank Aaron (Milwaukee) takes the batting title (.328) and gets 200 hits (the only major leaguer to do so in 1956). Stan Musial (St. Louis) wins the RBI title (109) and Willie Mays (New York) steals 40 bases.

REGULAR SEASON

American League
The New York Yankees (98-56) win their 3d pennant in a row, defeating Chicago by 8 games. Tom Sturdivant (16-6), Bobby Schantz (11-5, 2.45 ERA), Don Larsen (10-4) and Whitey Ford (11-5) are the aces in a pitching staff that leads the AL in ERA (3.00) and saves (42). Moose Skowron (.304, 88 RBI), Mickey Mantle (.365, 34 HRs, 94 RBI) and Yogi Berra (24 HRs, 82 RBI) pace the offense, which leads the AL in batting (.268).

National League
The Milwaukee Braves (95-59) win their first pennant as a Milwaukee franchise, beating out St. Louis by 8 games. Warren Spahn (21-11), Lew Burdette (17-9) and Bob Buhl (18-7) lead the Braves' pitching staff. Hank Aaron (.322, 44 HRs, 132 RBI) and Eddie Mathews (.292, 32 HRs, 94 RBI) supply the power for an offense that generates 100 home runs and 772 runs.

ALL-STAR GAME & WORLD SERIES

All-Star Game (St. Louis, NL)
The AL defeats the NL, 6-5, in a stirring 9th-inning finale in which each side scores 3 runs. Chicago's Minnie Minoso makes a sensational grab of a line drive off the bat of Gil Hodges (Brooklyn) to save the day for the AL.

World Series
In the 3d straight 7-game Series, Milwaukee defeats the New York Yankees, 4 games to 3, for its first world championship as a Milwaukee franchise. Lew Burdettte, with 3 complete game wins (allowing only 2 earned runs in 27 innings) is the Milwaukee star. Hank Aaron (.393) collects 11 hits and 7 RBI to lead the offense. Hank Bauer (6 RBI), Joe Coleman (.364) and Yogi Berra (.320) lead the Yankees.

AWARDS & HONORS

Hall of Fame Inductee
Sam Crawford

Most Valuable Players
AL: Mickey Mantle (New York)
NL: Hank Aaron (Milwaukee)

Rookies of the Year
AL: Tony Kubek (New York)
NL: Jack Sanford (Philadelphia)

Cy Young Award Winner
Warren Spahn (Milwaukee, NL)

AL Pitching Leaders
Jim Bunning (Detroit) and Billy Pierce (Chicago) each win 20 games. Bobby Schantz (Philadelphia) has the best ERA (2.45), and teammate Bob Grim is credited with the most saves (19). Early Wynn (Cleveland) strikes out 184. Bob Keegan (Chicago) hurls a no-hitter.

AL Batting & Base Running Leaders
Ted Williams (Boston), in his 16th season, leads the league in batting (.388). Roy Sievers (Washington) hits 42 home runs and has 114 RBI. Luis Aparicio (Chicago) repeats as the stolen-base champ (28).

NL Pitching Leaders
Warren Spahn (Milwaukee) leads in wins (21). Johnny Podres (Brooklyn) has the best ERA (2.66), and Jack Sanford (Philadelphia) fans 188. Clem Labine (Brooklyn) is credited with 17 saves.

NL Batting & Base Running Leaders
Hank Aaron (Milwaukee) smacks 44 home runs and drives home 132 to lead the NL. Stan Musial (St. Louis) wins his 6th batting title (.351). Willie Mays (New York) steals the most bases (38) and hits the most triples (20).

1958

REGULAR SEASON

American League
The New York Yankees (92-62) finish 10 full games ahead of Chicago to capture their 4th pennant in a row. Bob Turley, the only 20-game winner among AL pitchers (21-7), is the ace of the Yankee mound corps, which leads the AL in ERA (3.22) and shutouts (21). Ryne Duren (20 saves) is the #1 reliever. Mickey Mantle (.304, 42 HRs, 97 RBI) and Yogi Berra (22 HRs, 90 RBI) lead a potent offense that produces 164 home runs and a .268 batting average.

National League
Milwaukee (92-62) wins its 2d NL pennant in a row, beating out Pittsburgh by 8 games. Warren Spahn (22-11) and Lew Burdette (20- 10) repeat as the Braves' mound stars. Don McMahon (7-2, 8 saves) is the top relief man. Hank Aaron (.326, 30 HRs, 95 RBI) again leads the Braves at the plate.
[Note: During the off-season, the New York Giants and Brooklyn Dodgers move to San Francisco and Los Angeles, respectively.]

ALL-STAR GAME & WORLD SERIES

All-Star Game (Baltimore, AL)
In a game featuring 13 hits, all singles, the AL defeats the NL again, 4-3. Baltimore's Billy O'Dell hurls 3 perfect innings for the AL to preserve the win.

World Series
For the 2d straight year, New York and Milwaukee meet in the World Series, with the Yankees avenging their 1957 defeat, 4 games to 3. Bob Turley (2-1) stars on the mound for New York along with Ryne Duren and Don Larsen. In all, the Yankees staff compiles 56 strikeouts. Hank Bauer is the slugging star (.323, 4 HRs, 8 RBI). Gil McDougald (.321) and Moose Skowron (7 RBI) are also important run producers. Warren Spahn (2-1, 2.20 ERA) stars on the mound for Milwaukee in a losing cause. Red Schoendienst (.300), Hank Aaron (.333) and Bill Bruton (.412) are Milwaukee's batting stars. New York is the first team to win a World Series after being behind 3 games to 1.

AWARDS & HONORS

Hall of Fame Inductees
None

Most Valuable Players
AL: Jackie Jensen (Boston)
NL: Ernie Banks (Chicago)

Rookies of the Year
AL: Albie Pearson (Washington)
NL: Orlando Cepeda (San Francisco)

Cy Young Award Winner
Bob Turley (New York, AL)

AL Pitching Leaders
Whitey Ford (New York) registers a 2.01 ERA. Early Wynn (Chicago) strikes out 179. Ryne Duren (New York) has the most saves (20). Jim Bunning (Detroit) and Hoyt Wilhelm (Baltimore) pitch no-hitters.

AL Batting & Base Running Leaders
Ted Williams (Boston) takes the AL batting title for the 2d year in a row (and 6th time in his career). Mickey Mantle (New York) hits the most homers (42) and Jackie Jensen (Boston) leads in RBI (122). Luis Aparicio (Chicago) wins the base-stealing title for the 3d straight year (29).

NL Pitching Leaders
Stu Miller (San Francisco) chalks up the league's best ERA (2.47). Warren Spahn (Milwaukee) has the most wins (22, tied with Bob Friend of Pittsburgh). Sam Jones (St. Louis) fans 235 and Roy Face gets 20 saves for Pittsburgh.

NL Batting & Base Running Leaders
Richie Ashburn (Philadelphia) wins the NL batting title (.350) and has the most hits in the majors (215). Ernie Banks (Chicago) slams 47 home runs and knocks in 129 runs. Willie Mays (San Francisco) repeats as the base-stealing champ (31).

New York Yankee manager **Casey Stengel** with three of his brightest stars: (l. to r.) **Mickey Mantle, Yogi Berra** and **Hank Bauer.** © UPI

1959

REGULAR SEASON

American League
The Chicago White Sox (94-60) break New York's latest string of pennants, finishing 5 games ahead of Cleveland to win their first flag since 1919. Early Wynn (22-10) and Bob Shaw (18-6) anchor Chicago's pitching staff, with the support of relief specialists Gerry Staley (8-5, 14 saves) and Turk Lown (9-2, 15 saves). Nellie Fox (.306) and Sherm Lollar (22 HRs, 84 RBI) produce the runs.

National League
Los Angeles and Milwaukee end the regular season in a tie (86-68). The Dodgers win their first pennant (as a Los Angeles franchise) in a playoff, 2 games to 0. Don Drysdale (17-13), Roger Craig (11-5) and Johnny Podres (14-9) lead a strong pitching staff (1,077 strikeouts, 26 saves). Gil Hodges (25 HRs, 80 RBI), Duke Snider (.308, 23 HRs, 88 RBI) and Charlie Neal (19 HRs, 83 RBI) are the major run producers.

ALL-STAR GAMES & WORLD SERIES

[Note: Two All-Star games are played starting in 1959.]

All-Star Game #1 (Pittsburgh, NL)
The NL scores 4 runs in the 7th and 8th innings to defeat the AL, 5- 4. Al Kaline (Detroit) and Ed Mathews (Milwaukee) hit home runs.

All-Star Game #2 (Los Angeles, NL)
The AL, backed by 3 home runs, beats the NL, 5-3.

World Series
Los Angeles defeats Chicago, 4 games to 2. No pitcher on either side goes the distance for the first time in World Series history. Larry Sherry, who won only 7 games during the regular season, wins 2 Series games with an 0.71 ERA. Johnny Podres and Don Drysdale also register wins. Charlie Neal (.370, 6 RBI) and Gil Hodges (.391) lead the Dodger offense. Ted Kluszewski (.391, 3 HRs, 10 RBI) is the offensive star for Chicago. In game 5, three White Sox pitchers combine for a shutout, a Series record.

AWARDS & HONORS

Hall of Fame Inductee
Zack Wheat

Most Valuable Players
AL: Nellie Fox (Chicago)
NL: Ernie Banks (Chicago)

Rookies of the Year
AL: Bob Allison (Washington)
NL: Willie McCovey (San Francisco)

Cy Young Award Winner
Early Wynn (Chicago, AL)

AL Pitching Leaders
Early Wynn (Chicago) wins 22 games. Hoyt Wilhelm (Baltimore) has the lowest ERA (2.19) and Jim Bunning (Detroit) reels off the most strikeouts (201). Chicago's Turk Lown leads in saves (15).

AL Batting & Base Running Leaders
Harmon Killebrew (Washington) and Rocky Colavito (Cleveland) tie with 42 homers. Jackie Jensen (Boston) leads in RBI (112). Harvey Kuenn (Detroit) wins the batting championship (.353). Luis Aparicio (Chicago) wins the base-stealing crown (56).

NL Pitching Leaders
Sam Jones (San Francisco) has the lowest ERA (2.83) and ties two other pitchers with 21 wins. Don Drysdale (Los Angeles) registers the most strikeouts (242). Lindy McDaniel (St. Louis) and Don McMahon (Milwaukee) collect 15 saves. Harvey Haddix (Pittsburgh) spins a no-hitter for 12 innings, then loses both no-hitter and game in the 13th.

NL Batting & Base Running Leaders
Hank Aaron (Milwaukee) dominates NL hitters with the highest average (.355) and most hits (223). Teammate Eddie Mathews takes the home-run title (46), and Ernie Banks (Chicago) leads in RBI (143). Willie Mays is the stolen-base leader (27).

REGULAR SEASON

American League
The New York Yankees (97-57) regain the pennant they lost in 1959, finishing 8 games in front of Baltimore. Roger Maris (.283, 39 HRs, 112 RBI), Moose Skowron (.309, 26 HRs, 91 RBI) and Mickey Mantle (40 HRs, 94 RBI) are the heavy hitters for New York. Art Ditmar (15-9), Whitey Ford (12-9), Bob Turley (9-3), Jim Coates (13-3) and Bobby Schantz (11 saves) head a pitching staff that leads the AL in ERA (3.52), saves (42) and shutouts (16).

National League
The Pittsburgh Pirates (95-59) win their first pennant since 1927, finishing 7 games in front of Milwaukee. Bob Friend (18-12), Vernon Law (20-9), Vinegar Bend Mizell (13-5) and ace reliever Roy Face (10- 8, 24 saves) are the top pitchers. Roberto Clemente (.314, 94 RBI), Dave Stuart (23 HRs, 83 RBI), Dick Groat (.325) and Bob Skinner (86 RBI) supply the offensive punch (.276 team batting average).

ALL-STAR GAMES & WORLD SERIES

All-Star Game #1 (Kansas City, AL)
The NL wins, 5-3, as Willie Mays (San Francisco) connects for 3 hits and Pittsburgh's Roy Face stars in relief for the NL.

All-Star Game #2 (New York, AL)
The NL shuts out the AL, 6-0, slamming 4 home runs for all its runs.

World Series
Pittsburgh defeats the New York Yankees for its first world championship since 1925, 4 games to 3. Vernon Law (2-0) and Harvey Haddix (2-0) are the pitching heroes for the Pirates. The Yankee offense out-hits the Pirates, 91-60, and scores twice as many runs (55 to 27), but loses the Series when Pirate second baseman Bill Mazeroski hits a dramatic homer in the bottom of the 9th inning in game 7. Bobby Richardson sets a new Series record with 12 RBI as he and teammate Mickey Mantle (.400, 3 HRs, 11 RBI) lead all batters on both sides. New York's Whitey Ford (2-0) hurls 2 shutouts in a losing cause.

AWARDS & HONORS

Hall of Fame Inductees
None

Most Valuable Players
AL: Roger Maris (New York)
NL: Dick Groat (Pittsburgh)

Rookies of the Year
AL: Ron Hansen (Baltimore)
NL: Frank Howard (Los Angeles)

Cy Young Award Winner
Vernon Law (Pittsburgh, NL)

AL Pitching Leaders
Frank Baumann (Chicago) leads the AL in ERA (2.67). Jim Perry (Cleveland) and Chuck Estrada (Baltimore) tie for most wins (18). Jim Bunning (Detroit) strikes out 201. Mike Fornieles (Boston) and Johnny Klippstein (Cleveland) are both credited with 14 saves.

AL Batting & Base Running Leaders
Pete Runnels (Boston) bats .320 to lead the league. Mickey Mantle (New York) belts 40 home runs and scores 119 runs while teammate Roger Maris has 112 RBI. Luis Aparicio (Chicago) leads in stolen bases (51) for the 5th straight year.

NL Pitching Leaders
Ernie Broglio (St. Louis) and Warren Spahn (Milwaukee) tie for the most wins (21). Don Drysdale (Los Angeles) strikes out 246. Mike Mc-Cormick (San Francisco) has the best ERA (2.70). Lindy McDaniel (St. Louis) leads in games saved (26). Don Cardwell (Chicago), Lew Burdette and Warren Spahn (both from Milwaukee) pitch no-hitters.

NL Batting & Base Running Leaders
Dick Groat (Pittsburgh) bats .325 and Ernie Banks (Chicago) blasts 41 homers. Hank Aaron (Milwaukee) leads in RBI (126) and Maury Wills (Los Angeles) steals 50 bases.

1961

REGULAR SEASON

American League
The New York Yankees (109-53) win their 19th pennant in the last 26 seasons. Whitey Ford (25-4), Ralph Terry (16-3) and reliever Luis Arroyo (15-5, 29 saves) star on the mound. Roger Maris (142 RBI) slams 61 homers to break Babe Ruth's single-season home-run record. Mickey Mantle (.317, 54 HRs, 128 RBI) keeps pace to complete the major leagues' most powerful 1-2 punch. [Note: The Minnesota Twins (formerly Washington Senators) and the Los Angeles Angels become new AL franchises in 1961. The league also lengthens its season from 154 games to 162.]

National League
The Cincinnati Reds (93-61) beat out Los Angeles for the pennant by 4 games to win their first NL flag since 1940. Joey Jay (21-10), Jim O'-Toole (19-9) and relievers Jim Brosnan and Bill Henry (16 saves each) are the pitching aces. Frank Robinson (.323, 37 HRs, 124 RBI), Gene Freese (26 HRs, 87 RBI), Vada Pinson (.343, 87 RBI) and Gordy Coleman (26 HRs, 87 RBI) lead the offense.

ALL-STAR GAMES & WORLD SERIES

All-Star Game #1 (San Francisco, NL)
In a record-setting, error-filled game (7), the NL comes out on top, 5-4, when Roberto Clemente (Pittsburgh) drives home the winning run in the 10th inning.

All-Star Game #2 (Boston, AL)
The first tie game (1-1) in All-Star game history goes into the record books when heavy rains stop the game after 9 innings of play.

World Series
The New York Yankees win another world championship, beating the Cincinnati Reds, 4 games to 1. Whitey Ford wins 2 games by shutouts, increasing his all-time Series record of consecutive scoreless innings to 32 and the most Series wins to 9. Buddy Daley and Luis Arroyo are the other Yankee winners (both in relief). Bobby Richardson continues his World Series heroics (see 1960) with a .391 average. Hector Lopez (.333) drives in 7 runs and Johnny Blanchard (.400) belts 2 home runs for New York. Cincinnati is held to 13 runs in the Series.

AWARDS & HONORS

Hall of Fame Inductees
Max Carey, Billy Hamilton

Most Valuable Players
AL: Roger Maris (New York)
NL: Frank Robinson (Cincinnati)

Rookies of the Year
AL: Don Schwall (Boston)
NL: Billy Williams (Chicago)

Cy Young Award Winner
Whitey Ford (New York, AL)

AL Pitching Leaders
Whitey Ford's (New York) 25 wins are tops in the AL. Luis Arroyo (New York) saves 20 games. Dick Donovan (Washington) has the best ERA (2.40). Camilo Pascual (Minnesota) strikes out 221 and tosses 8 shutouts to lead the league.

AL Batting & Base Running Leaders
Norm Cash (Detroit) collects 193 hits and wins the batting title (.361). Roger Maris (New York) hits 61 home runs to break Babe Ruth's all-time single-season record. Maris also drives in the most runs (142). Luis Aparicio (Chicago) steals 53 bases.

NL Pitching Leaders
Warren Spahn (Milwaukee) tops all NL pitchers with a 3.02 ERA and ties Joey Jay (Cincinnati) for the most wins (21). He also hurls his 2d no-hitter in 2 years. Sandy Koufax (Los Angeles) strikes out 269. Stu Miller (San Francisco) and Roy Face (Pittsburgh) pick up 17 saves each.

NL Batting & Base Running Leaders
Orlando Cepeda (San Francisco) hits the most home runs (46) and drives home 142. Roberto Clemente (Pittsburgh) wins the batting title (.351). Maury Wills (Los Angeles) repeats as the #1 base stealer (35).

Roger Maris strokes his record–shattering 61st homer of the year into the right field stands at Yankee Stadium. The dramatic home run comes off Boston pitcher Tracy Stallard during the final game of the 1961 season (October 1). © National Baseball Library

1962

REGULAR SEASON

American League
The New York Yankee dynasty continues as New York (96-66) wins the AL pennant by 5 games over Minnesota. Ralph Terry (23-12), Whitey Ford (17-8), Bill Stafford (14-9) and relief ace Marshall Bridges (18 saves) are the pitching standouts. Yankee hitters lead the AL with a 2.67 average. Tom Tresh (20 HRs, 93 RBI), Roger Maris (33 HRs, 100 RBI), Elston Howard (21 HRs, 91 RBI) and Mickey Mantle (.321, 30 HRs, 89 RBI) are the top run producers.

National League
The San Francisco Giants and Los Angeles Dodgers end the season tied for first (101-61), but San Francisco wins the pennant in a playoff, 2 games to 1. Their pitching staff is led by Juan Marichal (18-11), Jack Sanford (24-7), Billy Pierce (16-6) and reliever Stu Miller (19 saves). Willie Mays (.304, 49 HRs, 141 RBI), Felipe Alou (.316, 25 HRs, 98 RBI) and Orlando Cepeda (.306, 35 HRs, 114 RBI) lead the Giant offense, which is #1 in the NL (.278 average, 204 HRs). [Note: Two new franchises, the Houston Astros and the New York Mets—led by ex-Yankee manager Casey Stengel—enter the NL. The season is extended from 154 games to 162.]

ALL-STAR GAMES & WORLD SERIES

All-Star Game #1 (Washington, AL)
The NL, led by Pittsburgh's Roberto Clemente and Maury Wills (Los Angeles), defeats the AL, 3-1.

All-Star Game #2 (Chicago, NL)
A 3-run homer in the 7th inning by Detroit's Rocky Colavito puts the game on ice for the AL, 9-4.

World Series
The New York Yankees defend their world championship successfully, beating San Francisco in a low-scoring Series, 4 games to 3. Ralph Terry (2-1) allows 5 runs over 25 innings. Whitey Ford and Bill Stafford win 1 game apiece for New York. Sluggers Mickey Mantle and Roger Maris are held to only 7 hits in 48 at-bats by the Giant staff. Rookie Tom Tresh hits .321 and scores 5 runs. The Giants' Chuck Hiller hits the NL's first grand-slam home run in a World Series game (#4). Bobby Richardson's grab of Willie McCovey's drive in the 9th inning of game 7 saves the game and clinches New York's 20th world championship.

AWARDS & HONORS

Hall of Fame Inductees
Bob Feller, Bill McKechnie, Jackie Robinson, Edd Roush

Most Valuable Players
AL: Mickey Mantle (New York)
NL: Maury Wills (Los Angeles

Rookies of the Year
AL: Tom Tresh (New York)
NL: Ken Hubbs (Chicago)

Cy Young Award Winner
Don Drysdale (Los Angeles, NL)

AL Pitching Leaders
Ralph Terry (New York) wins 23 games and Hank Aguirre (Detroit) turns in the best ERA (2.21). Camilo Pascual (Minnesota) fans 206 and Dick Radatz (Boston) picks up 24 saves. Four AL pitchers toss no-hitters during the 1962 season.

AL Batting & Base Running Leaders
Harmon Killebrew (Minnesota) paces the AL in home runs (48) and RBI (126). Pete Runnels (Boston) wins the batting title (.326) and Luis Aparicio (Chicago) leads in stolen bases (31) for the 7th straight year.

NL Pitching Leaders
Los Angeles Dodger pitchers Sandy Koufax and Don Drysdale dominate the NL's pitching records. Koufax has the lowest ERA (2.54) and throws his first no-hitter. Drysdale wins 25 and strikes out 232. Roy Face (Pittsburgh) is the top reliever with 28 saves.

NL Batting & Base Running Leaders
Tommy Davis (Los Angeles) leads the NL in RBI (153), hits (230) and batting average (.346). Willie Mays (San Francisco) slams 49 home runs. Maury Wills (Los Angeles) sets a new major league single- season record for stolen bases (104).

1963

REGULAR SEASON

American League
The New York Yankees (104-57) take their 4th pennant in a row and 14th in the last 17 years, ending the season 10½ games in front of Chicago. Whitey Ford (24-7), Jim Bouton (21-7) and reliever Hal Reniff (18 saves) are the mound leaders. Joe Pepitone (27 HRs, 89 RBI) and Elston Howard (28 HRs, 85 RBI) lead the hitting attack.

National League
The Los Angeles Dodgers (99-63) capture the NL flag by 6 games over St. Louis. Sandy Koufax (25-5, 1.88 ERA), Don Drysdale (19-17) and Ron Perranoski (21 saves, 1.67 ERA) lead the Dodger pitching staff, which has the NL's best ERA (2.85), most strikeouts (1,095) and most shutouts (24). Tommy Davis (.326, 16 HRs, 88 RBI) and Frank Howard (28 HRs) are the main run producers on a weak-hitting squad.

ALL-STAR GAME & WORLD SERIES

[Note: In 1963, the major leagues go back to playing only one All-Star game.]

All-Star Game (Cleveland, AL)
In celebration of Stan Musial's (St. Louis) 24th appearance in the All-Star game (a record), the NL defeats the AL, 5-3. Willie Mays (San Francisco) stars at bat, in the field, and on the base paths.

World Series
The Los Angeles Dodgers upset the New York Yankees in a clean sweep, 4 games to 0. Sandy Koufax (2-0), Don Drysdale (1-0) and Johnny Podres (1-0) overpower the Yankee hitters (combined 1.00 ERA). New York's 4 runs is the lowest output ever recorded in Series play. Tommy Davis (.400) is the only man on either side to get more than 5 hits.

AWARDS & HONORS

Hall of Fame Inductees
John Clarkson, Elmer Flick, Sam Rice, Eppa Rixey

Most Valuable Players
AL: Elston Howard (New York)
NL: Sandy Koufax (Los Angeles)

Rookies of the Year
AL: Gary Peters (Chicago)
NL: Pete Rose (Cincinnati)

Cy Young Award Winner
Sandy Koufax (Los Angeles, NL)

AL Pitching Leaders
Whitey Ford (New York) leads the AL in wins (24) and rookie Gary Peters (Chicago) has the best ERA (2.33). Camilo Pascual (Minnesota) strikes out 202. Stu Miller (Baltimore) saves 27.

AL Batting & Base Running Leaders
Carl Yastrzemski (Boston) tops all hitters with a .321 average and 183 hits. Teammate Dick Stuart collects 118 RBI. Harmon Killebrew (Minnesota) belts 45 homers. Luis Aparicio (Chicago) steals 40 bases.

NL Pitching Leaders
Sandy Koufax (Los Angeles) is only the 4th pitcher in major league history to strike out more than 300 batters in a season (306). He also ties Juan Marichal (San Francisco) for the most wins (25), hurls 11 shutouts, posts the best ERA (1.88) and throws his 2d no-hitter in 2 years. Lindy McDaniel (Chicago) saves 22 games for the Cubs.

NL Batting & Base Running Leaders
Tommy Davis (Los Angeles) repeats as batting champion (.326). Hank Aaron (Milwaukee) has the most RBI (130), and homers (44, tied with Willie McCovey of San Francisco). Maury Wills (Los Angeles) wins his 4th consecutive stolen-base title (40).

1964

REGULAR SEASON

American League
The New York Yankees (99-63), under new manager Yogi Berra, capture the flag by only 1 game over Chicago and 2 over Baltimore. Jim Bouton (18-13), Whitey Ford (17-6) and Al Downing (13-8) lead the pitching staff. Mickey Mantle (.303, 35 HRs, 111 RBI), Roger Maris (.281, 26 HRs, 71 RBI) and Joe Pepitone (28 HRs, 100 RBI) are the top run producers.

National League
The St. Louis Cardinals (93-69) win their first pennant since 1946 behind the strong pitching of Bob Gibson (19-12), Curt Simmons (18-9) and Ray Sadecki (20-11). Ken Boyer (.295, 24 HRs, 119 RBI) and Bill White (.303, 21 HRs, 102 RBI) are the power hitters.

ALL-STAR GAME & WORLD SERIES

All-Star Game (New York, NL)
The NL scores 4 runs in the last of the 9th, 3 on Johnny Callison's (Philadelphia) homer, to win 7-4.

World Series
In an exciting 7-game Series, the New York Yankees lose to St. Louis. Bob Gibson (2-1, 31 strikeouts) stars on the mound for the Cardinals. His catcher, Tim McCarver, bats .478 and drives in 5 runs to lead the offense. Lou Brock (.300) and Ken Boyer (2 HRs, 6 RBI) are also heavy contributors for St. Louis. Jim Bouton (2-0, 1.56 ERA) leads the Yankee staff. Bobby Richardson (.406) gets 13 hits in the Series to break his own record (12). Mickey Mantle (.333, 8 RBI) and Tom Tresh (2 HRs, 7 RBI) hit the ball well in a losing cause.

AWARDS & HONORS

Hall of Fame Inductees
Luke Appling, Red Faber, Burleigh Grimes, Miller Huggins, Tim Keefe, Heinie Manush, Monte Ward

Most Valuable Players
AL: Brooks Robinson (Baltimore)
NL: Ken Boyer (St. Louis)

Rookies of the Year
AL: Tony Oliva (Minnesota)
NL: Richie Allen (Philadelphia)

Cy Young Award Winner
Dean Chance (Los Angeles, AL)

AL Pitching Leaders
Dean Chance (Los Angeles) pitches 11 shutouts, has the lowest ERA (1.65) and the most wins (20, tied with Gary Peters of Chicago). Al Downing (New York) leads in strikeouts (217). Dick Radatz (Boston) is first in saves (29).

AL Batting & Base Running Leaders
Harmon Killebrew (Minnesota) slams 49 homers. Tony Oliva wins the batting title (.323) and collects the most hits (217). Brooks Robinson (Baltimore) drives in 118 runs and Luis Aparicio (Chicago) steals 57 bases.

NL Pitching Leaders
Sandy Koufax (Los Angeles) has the lowest ERA (1.74) and pitches a no-hitter for the 3d year in a row. Larry Jackson (Chicago) has the most wins (24), and Bob Veale (Pittsburgh) fans 250. Hal Woodeshick (Houston) is the top reliever (23 saves).

NL Batting & Base Running Leaders
Roberto Clemente (Pittsburgh) gets 211 hits and a .329 batting average to pace all NL hitters. Willie Mays (San Francisco) hits the most home runs (47), and Ken Boyer (St. Louis) is first in RBI (119). Maury Wills (Los Angeles) steals 53 bases.

REGULAR SEASON

American League
The Minnesota Twins (102-60) capture their first pennant, beating the White Sox by 7 games. Mudcat Grant (21-7), Kim Kaat (18-11), Jim Perry (12-7) and relief ace Al Worthington (21 saves) are the top hurlers. Tony Oliva (.321, 98 RBI), Jimmie Hall (.285, 20 HRs, 86 RBI) and Bob Allison (23 HRs, 78 RBI) provide the power.

National League
The Los Angeles Dodgers (97-65) regain the pennant they lost in 1964, finishing just 2 games in front of San Francisco. Sandy Koufax (26-8, 2.04 ERA) and Don Drysdale (23-12) account for half of the Dodgers' victories. No regular in the lineup bats over .300 and no one drives in more than 70 runs during the season.

Los Angeles Dodger ace **Sandy Koufax** wins his second straight Cy Young Award and pitches his fourth no–hitter in four years. © National Baseball Library

ALL-STAR GAME & WORLD SERIES

All-Star Game (Minnesota, AL)
The NL wins its 3d straight All-Star game, 6-5, in a slug-fest (5 HRs, 19 hits). A spectacular catch in the 8th inning by Willie Mays (San Francisco) stops an AL rally.

World Series
The Los Angeles Dodgers beat the Minnesota Twins, 4 games to 3, to regain the world championship they won in 1963. Sandy Koufax (2-1, 29 strikeouts) gives up only 1 run in 24 innings. Maury Wills (.367) and Ron Fairly (.379, 2 HRs, 6 RBI) lead the offense. The Twins, who are shut out 3 times in the Series, are led by Mudcat Grant on the mound (2-1) and Zoilo Versalles (.286) at bat.

AWARDS & HONORS

Hall of Fame Inductee
Pud Galvin

Most Valuable Players
AL: Zoilo Versalles (Minnesota)
NL: Willie Mays (San Francisco)

Rookies of the Year
AL: Curt Blefary (Baltimore)
NL: Jim Lefebre (Los Angeles)

Cy Young Award Winner
Sandy Koufax (Los Angeles, NL)

AL Pitching Leaders
Sam McDowell (Cleveland) leads the league in ERA (2.18) and strikeouts (325). Mudcat Grant (Minnesota) wins the most games (21). Ron Kline (Washington) is the top reliever (29 saves).

AL Batting & Base Running Leaders
Tony Oliva (Minnesota) repeats as the league leader in batting (.321). Tony Conigliaro (Boston) hits the most home runs (32). Rocky Colavito (Cleveland) drives in 108 runs. Bert Campaneris (Kansas City) is the base-stealing champ (51).

NL Pitching Leaders
Sandy Koufax (Los Angeles) posts the most wins (26), lowest ERA (2.04) and most strikeouts (382, a major league record). He also hurls a no-hitter for the 4th year in a row. Ted Abernathy (Chicago) registers the most saves (31). Jim Maloney (Cincinnati) pitches 2 no-hitters.

NL Batting & Base Running Leaders
Roberto Clemente (Pittsburgh) leads the AL in batting (.329). Willie Mays (San Francisco) collects the most home runs (52) and Deron Johnson (Cincinnati) has the most RBI (130). Maury Wills (Los Angeles) is the top base stealer (94).

1966

REGULAR SEASON

American League
The Baltimore Orioles (97-63) win their first AL pennant, finishing 9 games in front of Minnesota. Rookie Jim Palmer (15-10) is the only Baltimore pitcher to win 15 games. Relief artists Stu Miller and Eddie Fisher register a total of 31 saves. The Orioles' top hitters are Boog Powell (34 HRs, 109 RBI), Brooks Robinson (23 HRs, 100 RBI) and Frank Robinson (.316, 49 HRs, 122 RBI).

National League
The Los Angeles Dodgers (95-67) win their 3d pennant in 4 years, finishing 1½ games ahead of San Francisco. Sandy Koufax (27- 9), Claude Osteen (17-14) and relief ace Phil Regan (14-1, 21 saves) lead a strong pitching staff (2.42 ERA, 1,084 strikeouts, 52 complete games, 20 shutouts). No Dodger hits .300 or drives in more than 75 runs.

In his first season with the Baltimore Orioles, **Frank Robinson** wins the Triple Crown and becomes the first player to win the MVP Award in both leagues. © National Baseball Library

ALL-STAR GAME & WORLD SERIES

All-Star Game (St. Louis, NL)
The NL wins its 4th All-Star game in a row, 2-1, in 10 innings. The Dodgers' Maury Wills singles in the winning run.

World Series
The Baltimore Orioles surprise the baseball world by sweeping Los Angeles, the 1965 world champions, 4 games to 0. The Dodgers score a total of 2 runs, the fewest ever in Series play, and fail to score in 33 consecutive innings, also a record. Dave McNally, Jim Palmer, Wally Bunker and Moe Drabowsky win one game apiece for Baltimore and compile an astounding 0.50 ERA for the Series. Boog Powell is the only regular on either side to bat .300. The Oriole defense does not make an error, only the 2d team to do so in World Series history.

AWARDS & HONORS

Hall of Fame Inductee
Ted Williams

Most Valuable Players
AL: Frank Robinson (Baltimore)
NL: Roberto Clemente (Pittsburgh)

Rookies of the Year
AL: Tommy Agee (Chicago)
NL: Tommy Helms (Cincinnati)

Cy Young Award Winner
Sandy Koufax (Los Angeles, NL)

AL Pitching Leaders
Jim Kaat (Minnesota) leads the AL with 25 wins. Gary Peters (Chicago) has the lowest ERA (1.98) and Sam McDowell (Cleveland) leads in strikeouts (225). Kansas City reliever Jack Aker has 32 saves. Sonny Siebert (Chicago) pitches the only no-hitter in the major leagues during 1966.

AL Batting & Base Running Leaders
Frank Robinson (Baltimore) wins the Triple Crown by hitting .316 with 49 home runs and 122 RBI. Bert Campaneris (Kansas City) is the top base stealer (52) for the 2d straight year.

NL Pitching Leaders
Sandy Koufax (Los Angeles) has the most wins (27), most strikeouts (317) and lowest ERA (1.73). His teammate, Phil Regan, picks up the most saves (21).

NL Batting & Base Running Leaders
Hank Aaron (Atlanta) leads the home-run parade (44) and drives in 127. Matty Alou (Pittsburgh) hits .342. Lou Brock (St. Louis) steals 74 bases. Willie Mays (San Francisco) becomes the 2d all-time home-run slugger (535).

1967

REGULAR SEASON

American League

The Boston Red Sox (92-70) win their first pennant since 1946, beating out Detroit and Minnesota by 1 game and Chicago by 3 in one of the tightest pennant races ever. Jim Lonborg (22-9) is the Red Sox pitching ace. John Wyatt leads the bullpen brigade (20 saves). Carl Yastrzemski (.326, 44 HRs, 121 RBI) leads the Boston hitters, who compile the league's best team average (.255) and hit the most home runs (158).

National League

The St. Louis Cardinals (101-60) run away with the pennant by 10½ games over 2d place San Francisco. Bob Gibson (13-7), Steve Carlton (14-9) and Nelson Briles (14-5) lead a solid pitching staff. Orlando Cepeda (.325, 25 HRs, 111 RBI), Lou Brock (.299, 21 HRs, 76 RBI) and Mike Shannon (77 RBI) are the Cardinals' top run producers.

Carl Yastrzemski wins the Triple Crown and leads the Boston Red Sox to the AL pennant.
© National Baseball Library

ALL-STAR GAME & WORLD SERIES

All-Star Game (California, AL)

The NL beats the AL, 2-1, for the 5th straight time. The 15-inning game, longest in All-Star game history, features a record 30 strikeouts (including 6 in a row by Fergie Jenkins). Cincinnati's Tony Perez slams a home run in the 15th to break the tie.

World Series

The St. Louis Cardinals defeat the Boston Red Sox, 4 games to 3. Lou Brock is the hitting- (.414) and base-running star (7 steals) for St. Louis. Roger Maris (traded by the Yankees in 1967) bats .385, scores 8 runs, and collects 7 RBI. Bob Gibson wins 3 games (3 earned runs in 27 innings) and belts a homer in the 7th-game clincher. Jim Lonborg wins 2 games for Boston. Carl Yastrzemski bats .400 with 5 RBI and 3 home runs to pace the Red Sox attack

AWARDS & HONORS

Hall of Fame Inductees
Red Ruffing, Lloyd Waner

Most Valuable Players
AL: Carl Yastrzemski (Boston)
NL: Orlando Cepeda (St. Louis)

Rookies of the Year
AL: Rod Carew (Minnesota)
NL: Tom Seaver (New York)

Cy Young Award Winners
AL: Jim Lonborg (Boston)
NL: Mike McCormick (San Francisco)

AL Pitching Leaders
Jim Lonborg (Boston) fans 246 and ties Earl Wilson (Detroit) for most wins (22). Joe Horlen (Chicago) has the best ERA (2.06). Minnie Rojas (California) saves 27 games. Three no-hitters are pitched during 1967.

AL Batting & Base Running Leaders
Carl Yastrzemski (Boston) takes the Triple Crown by batting .326, collecting 121 RBI and tying Harmon Killebrew (Minnesota) for most home runs (44). Bert Campaneris (Kansas City) is the #1 base stealer (55) for the 3d straight year.

NL Pitching Leaders
Phil Niekro (Atlanta) chalks up the best ERA (1.87). Mike McCormick (San Francisco) has the most wins (22) and Jim Bunning (Philadelphia) leads in strikeouts (253). Ted Abernathy (Cincinnati) leads in games saved (28). Don Wilson (Houston) tosses the NL's only no-hitter during 1967.

NL Batting & Base Running Leaders
Roberto Clemente (Pittsburgh) wins his 3d batting title (.357) and collects the most hits (209). Hank Aaron (Atlanta) belts 39 homers and Orlando Cepeda (St. Louis) drives home 111. Lou Brock (St. Louis) leads all base stealers with 52.

REGULAR SEASON

American League
The Detroit Tigers (103-59) easily capture their first pennant since 1945, finishing 12 games ahead of Baltimore. Denny McLain (31-6) and Mickey Lolich (17-9) pace the Detroit mound staff. Willie Horton (.285, 36 HRs, 85 RBI), Bill Freehan (25 HRs, 84 RBI) and Jim Northrup (21 HRs, 90 RBI) lead the offense. [Note: The Kansas City franchise moves to Oakland, California, in 1968.]

National League
The St. Louis Cardinals (97-65) recapture the NL flag, defeating San Francisco by 9 games. Bob Gibson (22-9) repeats as the Cardinals' pitching ace, with Nelson Briles (19-11) and reliever Joe Hoerner (8- 2, 17 saves) in support. Curt Flood (.301) is the only regular to bat over .300 (team average is only .249).

Bob Gibson's ERA of 1.12 and 13 shutouts are the lowest figures in modern history. © National Baseball Library

ALL-STAR GAME & WORLD SERIES

All-Star Game (Houston, NL)
In the lowest-scoring game in All-Star history, the NL wins its 6th straight, 1-0. Tom Seaver (New York) fans 5 of the 6 batters he faces.

World Series
Detroit wins an exciting 7-game Series, defeating St. Louis, 4 games to 3, behind the great pitching of Mickey Lolich (3-0, 1.67 ERA) and the hitting of Al Kaline (.379, 2 HRs, 8 RBI). Norm Cash (.385, 5 RBI) and Jim Northrup (2 HRs, 8 RBI) are also heavy contributors. Bob Gibson (2-1, 1.67 ERA) is the pitching star for St. Louis, increasing his total Series victories to 7 (2d only to Whitey Ford's 9). Gibson also sets a new Series record of 35 strikeouts, including 17 in game 1 (also a Series record). Lou Brock (.464, 5 RBI, 7 steals) is the Cardinals' top hitter.

AWARDS & HONORS

Hall of Fame Inductees
Goose Goslin, Kiki Cuyler, Joe "Ducky" Medwick

Most Valuable Players
AL: Denny McLain (Detroit)
NL: Bob Gibson (St. Louis)

Rookies of the Year
AL: Stan Bahnsen (New York)
NL: Johnny Bench (Cincinnati)

Cy Young Award Winners
AL: Denny McLain (Detroit)
NL: Bob Gibson (St. Louis)

AL Pitching Leaders
Luis Tiant (Cleveland) turns in the lowest ERA (1.60). Denny McLain's (Detroit) 31 wins tops the majors. Sam McDowell (Cleveland) strikes out 283. Al Worthington (Minnesota) is the #1 relief ace (18 saves).

AL Batting & Base Running Leaders
Carl Yastrzemski (Boston) is the only AL batter to hit over .300 (.301). Teammate Ken Harrelson drives in 109 and Frank Howard (Washington) clubs 44 homers. Bert Campaneris (Oakland) leads in stolen bases (62).

NL Pitching Leaders
Bob Gibson's (St. Louis) 268 strikeouts and 1.12 ERA lead the NL. Juan Marichal (San Francisco) has the most wins (26). Phil Regan (Chicago/St. Louis) saves 25 games.

NL Batting & Base Running Leaders
Willie McCovey (San Francisco) leads the NL in home runs (36) and RBI (105). Pete Rose (Cincinnati) wins the batting title (.335) and collects the most hits (210, tied with Felipe Alou of Pittsburgh). Lou Brock (St. Louis) steals 62 bases.

1969

REGULAR SEASON

American League
[Note: The AL is divided into Eastern and Western divisions, and new franchises in Kansas City and Seattle join the AL West.]
AL East Baltimore (109-53) wins the division by a whopping 19-game margin. Jim Palmer (16-4), Mike Cuellar (23-11) and Dave McNally (20-7) head the mound corps. Frank Robinson (.308, 32 HRs, 100 RBI) and Boog Powell (.304, 37 HRs, 121 RBI) are the big run producers.
AL West Minnesota (97-65) wins behind the pitching of Jim Perry (20-6) and reliever Ron Perranoski (31 saves). Harmon Killebrew (49 HRs, 140 RBI) leads the Twins' attack.

National League
[Note: The NL is divided into Eastern and Western divisions. A new Montreal franchise joins the NL East, and San Diego joins NL West.]
NL East The New York Mets (100-62) win the division title behind the strong arms of Tom Seaver (25-7), Jerry Koosman (17-9) and relief ace Tug McGraw (12 saves). Tommy Agee (26 HRs, 76 RBI) and Cleon Jones (.340, 75 RBI) lead the offense.
NL West Atlanta (93-69) finishes 3 games ahead of San Francisco. Phil Niekro (23-13) is the ace of the Braves' pitching staff. Hank Aaron (.300, 44 HRs, 97 RBI) and Orlando Cepeda (22 HRs, 88 RBI) crank out the runs.

ALL-STAR GAME & POSTSEASON GAMES

All-Star Game (Washington, AL)
Baseball celebrates its 100th birthday in the nation's Capitol. The NL wins its 7th straight, 9-3, as Willie McCovey (San Francisco) blasts 2 homers.

AL Championship Series
Baltimore sweeps Minnesota, 3 games to 0. Paul Blair and Brooks Robinson pace the Oriole attack.

NL Championship Series
The New York Mets defeat Atlanta, 3 games to 0. Hank Aaron (Atlanta) slams 3 home runs in a losing cause.

World Series
The New York Mets complete their dream season, beating Baltimore, 4 games to 1, for their first world championship. Jerry Koosman (2-0) leads the Mets' mound staff, which allows only 9 runs (1.80 ERA) and 23 hits. Donn Clendenon (.357, 3 HRs), Al Weis (.455) and Ron Swoboda (.400) are the top Mets hitters. Mike Cuellar wins Baltimore's only game in the Series.

AWARDS & HONORS

Hall of Fame Inductees
Roy Campanella, Stan Coveleski, Waite Hoyt, Stan Musial

Most Valuable Players
AL: Harmon Killebrew (Minnesota)
NL: Willie McCovey (San Francisco)

Rookies of the Year
AL: Lou Piniella (Kansas City)
NL: Ted Sizemore (St. Louis)

Cy Young Award Winners
AL: Denny McLain (Detroit) and Mike Cuellar (Baltimore)
NL: Tom Seaver (New York)

AL Pitching Leaders
Dick Bosman's (Washington) ERA (2.19) leads the AL. Denny McLain (Detroit) hurls 9 shutouts and gets the most wins (24). Sam McDowell (Cleveland) leads in strikeouts (279). Ron Perranoski (Minnesota) saves 31 games.

AL Batting & Base Running Leaders
Harmon Killebrew (Minnesota) belts 49 homers and drives in 140. Teammate Rod Carew (.332 batting average) is also a league leader. Tommy Harper of Seattle tops all base stealers with 73 thefts.

NL Pitching Leaders
Tom Seaver (New York) leads the NL in wins (25). Juan Marichal (San Francisco) posts a 2.10 ERA. Fergie Jenkins (Chicago) fans 273. Fred Gladding (Houston) is the top relief specialist (29 saves).

NL Batting & Base Running Leaders
Willie McCovey (San Francisco) slaps out 45 homers and drives in 126. Pete Rose (Cincinnati) wins his 2d batting title (.348). Lou Brock (St. Louis) captures the stolen-base title (53) for the 4th straight year.

New York Met center fielder **Tommy Agee** makes one of his two spectacular catches in game 3 of the 1969 World Series (October 14). © National Baseball Library

1970

REGULAR SEASON

American League
AL East Baltimore (108-54) repeats as divison winner, with New York 15 games behind. The Oriole pitching staff features Jim Palmer (20-10, 2.71 ERA), Mike Cuellar (24-8) and Dave McNally (24-9). Boog Powell (.297, 35 HRs, 114 RBI), Brooks Robinson (94 RBI) and Frank Robinson (25 HRs, 78 RBI) are the big hitters.

AL West The Seattle franchise is moved to Milwaukee. The Minnesota Twins (98-64) win the AL West for the 2d year in a row. Jim Perry (24-12) and reliever Ron Perranoski (34 saves) again pace the mound staff. Harmon Killebrew (41 HRs, 113 RBI) and Tony Oliva (.325, 23 HRs, 107 RBI) star on offense.

National League
NL East The Pittsburgh Pirates (89-73) finish 5 games ahead of Chicago to win the division. A balanced pitching staff and the hitting of Roberto Clemente (.352), Bob Robertson (27 HRs, 82 RBI), Manny Sanguillen (.325) and Willie Stargell (31 HRs, 85 RBI) are key factors.

NL West The Cincinnati Reds (102-60) win the NL West by a comfortable 14½-game margin over Los Angeles. Relief ace Wayne Granger (35 saves), Gary Nolan (18-7), Jim Merritt (20-12) and Wayne Simpson (14-3) are the mound mainstays. Johnny Bench (.293, 45 HRs, 148 RBI), Tony Perez (.317, 40 HRs, 129 RBI) and Lee May (34 HRs, 94 RBI) spark the offense.

ALL-STAR GAME & POSTSEASON GAMES

All-Star Game (Cincinnati, NL)
In a 12-inning thriller, the NL wins its 8th All-Star contest in a row, 5-4.

AL Championship Series
Baltimore sweeps Minnesota, 3 games to 0. Boog Powell has 6 RBI as the Twins' pitching staff gives up 27 runs.

NL Championship Series
Cincinnati downs Pittsburgh, 3 games to 0, behind superb pitching (0.96 ERA).

World Series
Baltimore wins its 2d world championship, defeating Cincinnati, 4 games to 1, behind its "Big Three" pitching staff—Jim Palmer, Mike Cuellar and Dave McNally. Brooks Robinson (.429, 6 HRs), Paul Blair (.474) and Boog Powell (5 RBI) carry the offensive load. Robinson's brilliant defensive plays at third base are also important factors.

AWARDS & HONORS

Hall of Fame Inductees
Lou Boudrea, Earle Combs, Jesse Haines

Most Valuable Players
AL: Boog Powell (Baltimore)
NL: Johnny Bench (Cincinnati)

Rookies of the Year
AL: Thurman Munson (New York)
NL: Carl Morton (Montreal)

Cy Young Award Winners
AL: Jim Perry (Minnesota)
NL: Bob Gibson (St. Louis)

AL Pitching Leaders
Diego Segui (Oakland) has the best ERA (2.56). Dave McNally and Mike Cuellar (both from Baltimore) tie Minnesota's Jim Perry with 24 wins. Sam McDowell (Cleveland) strikes out 304. Ron Perranoski (Minnesota) saves 34 games.

AL Batting & Base Running Leaders
Frank Howard (Washington) leads in HRs (44) and RBI (126). Carl Yastrzemski (Boston) ties Alex Johnson (California) for the batting title (.329). Bert Campaneris (Oakland) takes the base-stealing title (42).

NL Pitching Leaders
Tom Seaver (New York) strikes out 283 and earns a 2.81 ERA. Bob Gibson (St. Louis) and Gaylord Perry (San Francisco) tie for the most wins (23). Wayne Granger (Cincinnati) picks up the most saves (35). Dock Ellis (Pittsburgh) and Bill Singer (Los Angeles) both spin no-hitters.

NL Batting & Base Running Leaders
Rico Carty (Atlanta) bats .366 to lead the NL. Johnny Bench (Cincinnati) cracks 45 homers and drives in 148. Bobby Tolan (Cincinnati) registers his first stolen-base title (57).

1971

REGULAR SEASON

American League
AL East Baltimore (101-57) keeps its division title as 4 pitchers—Jim Palmer, Mike Cuellar, Dave McNally and Pat Dobson —win 20 or more games each. Boog Powell (22 HRs, 92 RBI) and Brooks Robinson (20 HRs, 92 RBI) swing the heavy bats.
AL West Oakland (101-60) wins behind the pitching of Vida Blue (24-8), Catfish Hunter (21-11) and Chuck Dobson (15-5). Sal Bando (24 HRs, 94 RBI) and Reggie Jackson (32 HRs, 80 RBI) supply the power.

National League
NL East The Pittsburgh Pirates (97-65) repeat as champs. Willie Stargell (.295, 48 HRs, 125 RBI) and Roberto Clemente (.341, 86 RBI) lead the NL's best offense. Relief ace Dave Giusti earns 30 saves.
NL West San Francisco (90-72) edges out Los Angeles by 1 game for the division title. Gaylord Perry (16-12) and Juan Marichal (18- 11) lead the pitching staff. Bobby Bonds (33 HRs, 102 RBI) paces the hitting attack.

ALL-STAR GAME & POSTSEASON GAMES

All-Star Game (Detroit, AL)
The AL wins its first All-Star game since 1962. Frank Robinson (Baltimore) is the first player to hit home runs for each league.

AL Championship Series
Baltimore sweeps Oakland, 3 games to 0. The Oriole pitchers—Jim Palmer, Mike Cuellar and Dave McNally—handcuff the A's, who score only 7 runs. Boog Powell (Baltimore) and Reggie Jackson (Oakland) each hit 2 home runs.

NL Championship Series
Pittsburgh defeats San Francisco, 3 games to 1. The Pirates connect for 8 home runs (4 by Bob Robertson) and outscore the Giants, 24 to 15. Willie McCovey slams 2 homers and drives home 6 to lead the Giants.

World Series
In a close 7-game Series, Pittsburgh surprises Baltimore, 4 games to 3, by out-hitting and outfielding the 1970 world champions. Steve Blass (2-0) gives up 1 earned run in 18 innings. Roberto Clemente (.414, 2 HRs) and Manny Sanguillen (.379) are the Pirates' big guns. Game 4 is the first World Series night game in history.

AWARDS & HONORS

Hall of Fame Inductees
Dave Bancroft, Jake Beckley, Chick Hafey, Harry Hooper, Joe Kelley, Rube Marquard, Satchel Paige

Most Valuable Players
AL: Vida Blue (Oakland)
NL: Joe Torre (St. Louis)

Rookies of the Year
AL: Chris Chambliss (Cleveland)
NL: Earl Williams (Atlanta)

Cy Young Award Winners
AL: Vida Blue (Oakland)
NL: Fergie Jenkins (Chicago)

AL Pitching Leaders
Vida Blue (Oakland) has the best ERA (1.82). Mickey Lolich (Detroit) posts the most wins (25) and strikeouts (308). Ken Sanders (Milwaukee) saves 31 games.

AL Batting & Base Running Leaders
Tony Oliva (Minnesota) wins the batting title for the 3d time (.337). Bill Melton (Chicago) belts 33 homers, and Harmon Killebrew (Minnesota) drives in 119 runs. Amos Otis (Kansas City) steals 52 bases.

NL Pitching Leaders
Ferguson Jenkins (Chicago) picks up the most wins (24). Tom Seaver (New York) produces the lowest ERA (1.76) and the most strikeouts (289). Dave Giusti (Pittsburgh) is the #1 relief man (30 saves). Ken Holtzman and Milt Pappas (both from Chicago) hurl no-hitters.

NL Batting & Base Running Leaders
Joe Torre (St. Louis) leads all NL hitters with a .363 average, 137 RBI and 230 hits. Pittsburgh's Willie Stargell crushes 48 home runs. Lou Brock (St. Louis) repeats as the top base stealer (64).

REGULAR SEASON

[Note: The 1972 season is shortened by the first major league players' strike in baseball history.]

American League

AL East Detroit (86-70) sneaks past Boston by ½ game to win the division. Mickey Lolich (22-14), Joe Coleman (19-14) and Woodie Fryman (10-3) are the pitching stars. A good defense offsets a weak offense (.237 BA).

AL West Oakland (93-62) repeats as champs. Leading pitchers are Catfish Hunter (21-7), Blue Moon Odom (15-6) and Ken Holtzman (19-11). Oakland's high-powered offense, led by Reggie Jackson and Mike Epstein, produces 134 home runs. [Note: Milwaukee switches to the AL East division and the Washington franchise becomes the Texas Rangers of the AL West division.]

National League

NL East The Pittsburgh Pirates (96-59) repeat as champions. Steve Blass (19-8) is the star pitcher and Willie Stargell (33 HRs, 112 RBI) is the top slugger.

NL West Cincinnati (95-59) captures the division by 10½ games. Clay Carroll's relief pitching (37 saves) and Johnny Bench's slugging (40 HRs, 125 RBI) are key factors in Cincinnati's success.

ALL-STAR GAME & POSTSEASON GAMES

All-Star Game (Atlanta, NL)

The NL wins 4-3, scoring the winning run in the 10th inning. (The NL has won all 7 extra-inning All-Star games.) Atlanta's Hank Aaron belts a home run in his home ball park.

AL Championship Series

Oakland defeats Detroit, 3 games to 2, led by pitchers Blue Moon Odom (2-0, 0.00 ERA) and Rollie Fingers (1-0, 1.69 ERA). Matty Alou (.381) is the hitting star for Oakland.

NL Championship Series

The Cincinnati Reds beat Pittsburgh, 3 games to 2, behind the steady hitting of Pete Rose (.450), Joe Morgan (2 HRs) and Johnny Bench (.333).

World Series

Oakland wins its first world championship, defeating Cincinnati, 4 games to 3. Catfish Hunter (2-0) and Ken Holtzman (1-0) star on the mound for the A's. Gene Tenace, Oakland's unheralded catcher, is the first player to hit home runs in his first 2 at-bats in World Series play (game #1). Tenace goes on to drive in 9 runs, more than half of his team's total. Cincinnati pitchers Ross Grimsley (2-1) and Jack Billingham (1-0, 1 save) excel in a losing cause.

AWARDS & HONORS

Hall of Fame Inductees

Yogi Berra, Josh Gibson, Lefty Gomez, Sandy Koufax, Buck Leonard, Early Wynn, Ross Youngs

Most Valuable Players

AL: Richie Allen (Chicago)
NL: Johnny Bench (Cincinnati)

Rookies of the Year

AL: Carlton Fisk (Boston)
NL: Jon Matlack (New York)

Cy Young Award Winners

AL: Gaylord Perry (Cleveland)
NL: Steve Carlton (Philadelphia)

AL Pitching Leaders

Nolan Ryan (California) registers 329 strikeouts and 9 shutouts to lead the AL. Luis Tiant (Boston) has the best ERA (1.91). Gaylord Perry (Cleveland) and Wilbur Wood (Chicago) register the most wins (24). Sparky Lyle (New York) is the top reliever (35 saves).

AL Batting & Base Running Leaders

Richie Allen (Chicago) belts 37 home runs and drives in 113. Rod Carew (Minnesota) wins his 2d batting title (.318). Bert Campaneris (Oakland) wins his 6th base-stealing title (52).

NL Pitching Leaders

Steve Carlton (Philadelphia) wins 27 games for his last-place team, strikes out 310, and records the lowest ERA (1.97). Burt Hooton and Milt Pappas (both from Chicago) pitch no-hit, no-run games. Clay Carroll (Cincinnati) leads in saves (37).

NL Batting & Base Running Leaders

Billy Williams (Chicago) is the batting champ (.333). Johnny Bench (Cincinnati) clouts 40 homers and drives in 125 runs. Lou Brock (St. Louis) steals 63 bases.

Pittsburgh Pirate **Roberto Clemente** strokes the 3,000th and final hit of his brilliant career (September 30). Three months later, he dies in a plane crash while bringing relief to Nicaraguan earthquake victims. © National Baseball Library

1973

REGULAR SEASON

American League
AL East Baltimore (97-65) regains the division title it lost to Detroit in 1972. The Oriole pitching staff, led by Jim Palmer (22-9), has the best ERA (3.07) in the AL.

AL West Oakland wins its 3d consecutive title behind Ken Holtzman (21-13), Vida Blue (20-9), Catfish Hunter (21-5) and Rollie Fingers (22 saves). Reggie Jackson (32 HRs, 117 RBI) and Sal Bando (29 HRs, 98 RBI) lead the offense. [Note: The AL introduces the designated hitter (DH) in 1973.]

National League
NL East The New York Mets (82-79) edge out St. Louis by 1½ games. Their pitching staff, led by Tom Seaver (19-10) and relief ace Tug McGraw (25 saves), registers 1,027 strikeouts. The team batting average (.246) is the lowest in the NL.

NL West Cincinnati (99-63) repeats as champs behind run producers Pete Rose (.338), Tony Perez (.314, 27 HRs, 101 RBI) and Johnny Bench (25 HRs, 104 RBI). Don Gullett (18-8) and Jack Billingham (19-10) are the pitching standouts.

ALL-STAR GAME & POSTSEASON GAMES

All-Star Game (Kansas City, AL)
The NL defeats the AL, 7-1, as a record number of players (54) compete. It is the NL's 10th win in the last 11 All-Star games.

AL Championship Series
Oakland downs Baltimore, 3 games to 2. Catfish Hunter (2-0) and Ken Holtzman (1-0) outpitch the Orioles. Bert Campaneris bats .333 and steals 3 bases for Oakland.

NL Championship Series
The New York Mets defeat Cincinnati, 3 games to 2. Tom Seaver (1-1, 17 strikeouts), Jerry Koosman (1-0) and Jon Matlack (1-0) hold the Reds' power hitters to only 8 runs in 5 games.

World Series
Oakland retains its world championship, beating the New York Mets, 4 games to 3. Errors (10) and weak hitting (.253 BA) undo the Mets. Ken Holtzman (2-1) and Catfish Hunter (1-0) lead the A's pitching staff. Reggie Jackson (.310, 6 RBI) is Oakland's leading hitter. Rusty Staub (.423, 6 RBI) is the offensive star for New York.

AWARDS & HONORS

Hall of Fame Inductees
Roberto Clemente, Monte Irvin, George Kelly, Warren Spahn, Mickey Welch

Most Valuable Players
AL: Reggie Jackson (Oakland)
NL: Pete Rose (Cincinnati)

Rookies of the Year
AL: Al Bumbry (Baltimore)
NL: Gary Matthews (San Francisco)

Cy Young Award Winners
AL: Jim Palmer (Baltimore)
NL: Tom Seaver (New York)

AL Pitching Leaders
Wilbur Wood (Chicago) has the most wins (24). Jim Palmer's (Baltimore) ERA (2.40) leads the AL. Nolan Ryan (California) strikes out 383, a new major league record. He also pitches 2 no-hit games. John Hiller (Detroit) has 38 saves.

AL Batting & Base Running Leaders
Reggie Jackson (Oakland) has the most home runs (32) and RBI (117). Rod Carew (Minnesota) repeats as the batting champ (.350) and collects the most hits (203). Tommy Harper (Boston) leads in stolen bases (54).

NL Pitching Leaders
Tom Seaver (New York) leads the NL in ERA (2.08) and strikeouts (251). Ron Bryant (San Francisco) wins the most games (24) and Mike Marshall (Montreal) earns the most saves (31).

NL Batting & Base Running Leaders
Willie Stargell (Pittsburgh) hits 44 home runs and drives in 119. Pete Rose (Cincinnati) wins the batting title (.338) and raps out the most hits (230). Lou Brock (St. Louis) steals 70 bases (and steals 50 or more for the 9th consecutive year, breaking Ty Cobb's record).

1974

REGULAR SEASON

American League
AL East Baltimore (91-71) wins its 3d title in 4 years behind the pitching of Mike Cuellar (22-10), Dave McNally (16-10) and Ross Grimsley (18-13). No player bats .300.
AL West Oakland (90-72) grabs its 4th straight title. Catfish Hunter (25-12), Vida Blue (17- 15) and Ken Holtzman (19-17) head the mound staff. Sal Bando (22 HRs, 103 RBI), Reggie Jackson (29 HRs, 93 RBI) and Joe Rudi (22 HRs, 99 RBI) control the offense.

National League
NL East Pittsburgh (88-74) takes its 4th title in 5 years, despite a mediocre pitching staff. Richie Zisk (.313, 100 RBI), Al Oliver (.321, 85 RBI) and Willie Stargell (.301, 25 HRs, 96 RBI) are the Pirates' leading hitters.
NL West Los Angeles (102-60) captures its first division championship. Don Sutton (19-9) and Andy Messersmith (20-6) are the new Dodger pitching aces. Mike Marshall delivers 21 saves. Jimmy Wynn (32 HRs, 108 RBI), Steve Garvey (.312, 21 HRs, 111 RBI) and Ron Cey (97 RBI) lead the attack.

Hank Aaron hits home run #715 to pass Babe Ruth and become baseball's all–time homerun king (April 4). Aaron, who finishes his career with a total of 755 homers, is elected to the Hall of Fame in 1982. © National Baseball Library

ALL-STAR GAME & POSTSEASON GAMES

All-Star Game (Pittsburgh, NL)
The NL continues its dominance, beating the AL again, 7-3. Newcomer Steve Garvey (Los Angeles) stars at bat and in the field.

AL Championship Series
Oakland grabs its 4th AL pennant, beating Baltimore, 3 games to 1. Only 18 runs are scored as both teams bat under .200 for the Series. Ray Fosse (.333) of Oakland is the only regular on either team to bat over .300.

NL Championship Series
Los Angeles defeats Pittsburgh, 3 games to 1. Don Sutton (2-0) tames the Pirate bats. Steve Garvey (.389, 2 HRs, 5 RBI) and Bill Russell (.389) lead the Dodger offense.

World Series
Oakland wins its 3d consecutive world championship, beating Los Angeles, 4 games to 1. Relief ace Rollie Fingers is credited with 3 saves and a win for Oakland. Ken Holtzman, Catfish Hunter and Blue Moon Odom are also winners, limiting the Dodgers to only 11 runs in 5 games. Joe Rudi (.333) and Bert Campaneris (.353) lead the Oakland attack.

AWARDS & HONORS

Hall of Fame Inductees
James "Cool Papa" Bell, Jim Bottomley, Whitey Ford, Bucky Harris, Mickey Mantle, Casey Stengel, Sam Thompson

Most Valuable Players
AL: Jeff Burroughs (Texas)
NL: Steve Garvey (Los Angeles)

Rookies of the Year
AL: Mike Hargrove (Texas)
NL: Bake McBride (St. Louis)

Cy Young Award Winners
AL: Catfish Hunter (Oakland)
NL: Mike Marshall (Los Angeles)

AL Pitching Leaders
Catfish Hunter (Oakland) leads the AL in ERA (2.49) and wins (25, tied with Ferguson Jenkins (Texas). Nolan Ryan (California) fans 367 and hurls his 3d no-hitter. Terry Forster (Chicago) registers 24 saves.

AL Batting & Base Running Leaders
Richie Allen (Chicago) smacks 32 home runs. Rod Carew (Minnesota) gets 218 hits and earns his 4th batting title (.364). Jeff Burroughs (Texas) has 118 RBI. Billy North (Oakland) has 54 steals.

NL Pitching Leaders
Andy Messersmith (Los Angeles) and Phil Niekro (Atlanta) tie for the most wins (20). Buzz Capra (Atlanta) heads the ERA list (2.28), and Steve Carlton (Philadelphia) strikes out 240. Mike Marshall (Los Angeles) appears in a record 106 games and saves 21 of them.

NL Batting & Base Running Leaders
In only his 2d year in the majors, Mike Schmidt (Philadelphia) leads the NL in home runs (36). Ralph Garr (Atlanta) bats .353 and has the most hits (214). Johnny Bench (Cincinnati) drives in 120 runs.

1975

REGULAR SEASON

American League
AL East The Boston Red Sox (95-65) win their first division title with good pitching from Rick Wise (19-12), Bill Lee (17-9) and Roger Moret (14-3). Rookies Fred Lynn (.331, 21 HRs, 105 RBI) and Jim Rice (.309, 22 HRs, 102 RBI) lead the AL's best offense (.275 BA).

AL West Oakland (98-64) wins the division for the 5th straight time. Vida Blue (22-11), Ken Holtzman (18-14) and Dick Bosman (11-4) are the pitching aces. The offense features Reggie Jackson (36 HRs, 104 RBI) and Gene Tenace (29 HRs, 87 RBI).

National League
NL East Pittsburgh (92-69) wins its 5th title in the last 6 years. Jerry Reuss (18-11) and reliever Dave Giusti (17 saves) star on the mound. Dave Parker (.308, 25 HRs, 101 RBI) and Willie Stargell (.295, 22 HRs, 90 RBI) are the big run producers.

NL West Cincinnati (108-54) easily takes the division with 6 different pitchers winning 10 or more games. Tony Perez (20 HRs, 109 RBI), Johnny Bench (28 HRs, 110 RBI) and Joe Morgan (.327, 94 RBI) provide the heavy hitting.

Boston's **Fred Lynn** becomes the first player in baseball history to win the Rookie of the Year and MVP awards in the same season.
© National Baseball Library

ALL-STAR GAME & POSTSEASON GAMES

All-Star Game (Milwaukee, AL)
The NL scores 3 runs in the 9th inning to whip the AL again, 6-3. Boston's Carl Yastrzemski crunches a 3-run homer to account for all AL runs.

AL Championship Series
Boston upsets the world champion Oakland A's in 3 straight games. Red Sox pitchers Luis Tiant and Rick Wise and other staff members hold the A's sluggers to 7 runs and 19 hits. Carlton Fisk and Carl Yastrzemski lead the Boston attack.

NL Championship Series
Cincinnati sweeps the Pittsburgh Pirates, 3 games to 0. Strong pitching by Don Gullett, Fred Norman and Gary Nolan, along with the bats of Tony Perez (.417) and Ken Griffey (.333), are the key factors.

World Series
Cincinnati wins its first world championship since 1940, beating Boston, 4 games to 3. The Reds score the winning run with 2 outs in the 9th inning of game 7. Rawley Eastwick wins 2 games in relief and Tony Perez drives in 7 runs with 3 homers. Pete Rose hits .400. For Boston, Luis Tiant (2-0, 12 strikeouts) stars on the mound. The Boston offense, led by Carl Yastrzemski, Fred Lynn and Carlton Fisk, outhits the Reds but loses the Series.

AWARDS & HONORS

Hall of Fame Inductees
Earl Averill, Billy Herman, Judy Johnson, Ralph Kiner

Most Valuable Players
AL: Fred Lynn (Boston)
NL: Joe Morgan (Cincinnati)

Rookies of the Year
AL: Fred Lynn (Boston)
NL: John Montefusco (San Francisco)

Cy Young Award Winners
AL: Jim Palmer (Baltimore)
NL: Tom Seaver (New York)

AL Pitching Leaders
Jim Palmer (Baltimore) has the lowest ERA (2.09) and the most wins (23, tied with Catfish Hunter of New York). Frank Tanana (California) fans 269. Goose Gossage (Chicago) has 26 saves. Nolan Ryan (California) pitches his 4th no-hitter in 3 years, a major league record.

AL Batting & Base Running Leaders
George Scott (Milwaukee) leads in RBI (109) and home runs (36, tied with Reggie Jackson of Oakland). Mickey Rivers (California) steals 70 bases. Rod Carew (Minnesota) is the batting champ (.359) for the 5th time.

NL Pitching Leaders
Tom Seaver (New York) wins 22 games and strikes out 243. Randy Jones (San Diego) leads the NL with a 2.24 ERA. Al Hrabosky (St. Louis) and Rawley Eastwick (Cincinnati) each have 22 saves. Ed Halicki (San Francisco) spins the NL's only no-hitter.

NL Batting & Base Running Leaders
Mike Schmidt (Philadelphia) is the home-run king (38) and teammate Greg Luzinski has the most RBI (120). Bill Madlock wins the batting title for Chicago (.354) and Davey Lopes (Los Angeles) steals 77 bases.

1976

REGULAR SEASON

American League
AL East The New York Yankees (97-62) win their first division title behind the pitching of Catfish Hunter (17-15), Dock Ellis (17- 8), Ed Figueroa (19-10) and reliever Sparky Lyle (23 saves). Graig Nettles (32 HRs, 93 RBI), Chris Chambliss (96 RBI) and Thurman Munson (.302, 105 RBI) lead the Yankee attack.
AL West Kansas City (90-72) wins its first division title. Dennis Leonard (17-10) and Al Fitzmorris (15-11) lead the pitching staff. George Brett (.333), John Mayberry (95 RBI) and Amos Otis (86 RBI) are the hitting stars.

National League
NL East Philadelphia (101-61) takes the division for the first time. Steve Carlton (20-7), Jim Lonborg (18-10) and 3 relievers with 36 combined saves lead the pitching corps. Mike Schmidt (38 HRs, 107 RBI) is the Phillies' top power hitter.
NL West Cincinnati (102-60) captures its 5th division championship in 7 years. George Foster (.306, 29 HRs, 121 RBI) and Joe Morgan (.320, 27 HRs, 111 RBI) spark the offense. No pitcher wins more than 15 games. Relief ace Rawley Eastwick saves 26 games.

ALL-STAR GAME & POSTSEASON GAMES

All-Star Game (Philadelphia, NL)
The NL routs the AL, 7-1, for its 5th straight win and 13 of the last 14 games. Cincinnati's George Foster and Cesar Cedeño (Houston) clout round-trippers.

AL Championship Series
The New York Yankees defeat Kansas City, 3 games to 2. Heavy hitting by Chris Chambliss (.524, 2 HRs, 8 RBI) and Thurman Munson (.435) pace New York's offense. Catfish Hunter, Dock Ellis and reliever Dick Tidrow are the winning pitchers.

NL Championship Series
Cincinnati defeats Philadelphia, 3 games to 0. Pete Rose (.429) and Ken Griffey (.385) lead the Reds' attack. Jay Johnstone of the Phillies bats .770 to lead all hitters. No pitcher on either side goes the distance.

World Series
Cincinnati sweeps New York, 4 games to 0, for its 2d straight world championship. The Reds' pitchers, led by Don Gullett, Pat Zachry and Gary Nolan, allow only 2 earned runs per game. Johnny Bench (.533, 2 HRs, 6 RBI) has the hot bat for Cincinnati. Thurman Munson (.529) is the Yankees' leading hitter.

AWARDS & HONORS

Hall of Fame Inductees
Oscar Charleston, Roger Connor, Cal Hubbard, Bob Lemon, Fred Lindstrom, John Henry Lloyd, Robin Roberts

Most Valuable Players
AL: Thurman Munson (New York)
NL: Joe Morgan (Cincinnati)

Rookies of the Year
AL: Mark Fidrych (Detroit)
NL: Pat Zachry (Cincinnati)
Butch Metzger (San Diego)

Cy Young Award Winners
AL: Jim Palmer (Baltimore)
NL: Randy Jones (San Diego)

AL Pitching Leaders
Rookie Mark Fidrych (Detroit) has the lowest ERA (2.34). Nolan Ryan (California) strikes out 327 and Jim Palmer (Baltimore) wins 22 games. Sparky Lyle's (New York) 23 saves lead the league.

AL Batting & Base Running Leaders
George Brett (Kansas City) wins the AL batting title (.333) and collects the most hits (215). Lee May (Baltimore) has 109 RBI. Graig Nettles (New York) slams 32 homers. Billy North (Oakland) steals 75 bases.

NL Pitching Leaders
Randy Jones (San Diego) posts the most wins (22). John Denny (St. Louis) leads the NL with a 2.52 ERA. Rawley Eastwick (Cincinnati) saves 26 games, and Tom Seaver (New York) strikes out 235.

NL Batting & Base Running Leaders
Bill Madlock (Chicago) wins his 2d batting championship (.339). Mike Schmidt (Philadelphia) hits 38 home runs (including 4 in one game). George Foster (Cincinnati) drives in 121. Davey Lopes (Los Angeles) takes the base-stealing title (63).

REGULAR SEASON

American League
AL East The New York Yankees (100-62), led by manager Billy Martin, repeat as division winners. Reggie Jackson (32 HRs, 110 RBI), Graig Nettles (37 HRs, 107 RBI), Chris Chambliss (90 RBI) and Thurman Munson (.308, 100 RBI) are the big run producers. Ron Guidry (16-7), Don Gullett (14-4), Ed Figueroa (16-11) and reliever Sparky Lyle (26 saves) lead the Yankee mound staff.
AL West Kansas City (102- 60) wins its 2d title. Dennis Leonard (20-12), Jim Colborn (18-14) and Paul Splitorff (16-6) are pitching standouts for the Royals. Al Cowens (.312, 23 HRs, 112 RBI), Hal McRae (.298, 21 HRs, 92 RBI) and George Brett (.312, 22 HRs, 88 RBI) are Kansas City's top batsmen.

National League
NL East Philadelphia (101-61) wins its 2d straight crown behind pitchers Steve Carlton (23-10), Larry Christenson (19-6) and relievers Ron Reed and Gene Garber (34 saves combined). Greg Luzinski (.309, 39 HRs, 130 RBI) and Mike Schmidt (38 HRs, 101 RBI) supply the power.
NL West Los Angeles (98-64) takes its 2d title. Starters Tommy John (20-7), Don Sutton (14-8), Rick Rhoden (16-10) and reliever Charlie Hough (27 saves) are the pitching aces. Steve Garvey (.297, 33 HRs, 115 RBI), Ron Cey (30 HRs, 110 RBI), Reggie Smith (.307, 32 HRs, 87 RBI) and Dusty Baker (30 HRs, 86 RBI) produce the runs for the Dodgers.

ALL-STAR GAME & POSTSEASON GAMES

All-Star Game (New York, AL)
Despite a 2-run rally in the 9th by the AL, the NL holds on to win its 6th straight, 7-5. Baltimore's ace Jim Palmer is rocked with a 4- run NL burst in the 1st inning.

AL Championship Series
The New York Yankees win their 2d straight pennant beating Kansas City, 3 games to 2. Sparky Lyle notches 2 wins in relief for New York. Mickey Rivers (.391) and Thurman Munson (5 RBI) lead the offense. Freddie Patek (.389, 5 RBI) and Hal McRae (.444, 6 runs scored) are the big hitters for Kansas City.

NL Championship Series
The Los Angeles Dodgers beat Philadelphia, 3 games to 1, in a low-scoring Series. The Dodger staff, led by Tommy John and Don Sutton, throttles the Philly batters. Dusty Baker (.357, 2 HRs, 8 RBI) is the hitting star for Los Angeles.

World Series
New York wins its first world championship since 1962, defeating Los Angeles, 4 games to 2. Mike Torrez (2-0, 15 strikeouts) and Ron Guidry (1-0) star on the mound for New York. Reggie Jackson (.450, 5 HRs, 8 RBI) is the hitting hero. In the final game, Jackson hits 3 homers in successive times at bat on the first pitch.

Lou Brock of the St. Louis Cardinals passes Ty Cobb to become baseball's all–time leader in stolen bases (September 10). With 893 career stolen bases, Brock is elected to the Hall of Fame in 1985. © National Baseball Library

AWARDS & HONORS

Hall of Fame Inductees
Ernie Banks, Martin DiHigo, Al Lopez, Amos Rusie, Joe Sewell

Most Valuable Players
AL: Rod Carew (Minnesota)
NL: George Foster (Cincinnati)

Rookies of the Year
AL: Eddie Murray (Baltimore)
NL: Andre Dawson (Montreal)

Cy Young Award Winners
AL: Sparky Lyle (New York)
NL: Steve Carlton (Philadelphia)

AL Pitching Leaders
Frank Tanana (California) records 7 shutouts and a 2.54 ERA. Relief ace Bill Campbell (Boston) saves 31 games. Nolan Ryan (California) strikes out 341.

AL Batting & Base Running Leaders
Jim Rice (Boston) clouts 39 home runs. Rod Carew (Minnesota) wins his 6th batting title (.388). He also gets the most hits (239) and scores the most runs (128). Larry Hisle (Minnesota) leads in RBI (119). Freddie Patek (Kansas City) wins his first stolen-base crown (53).

NL Pitching Leaders
John Candelaria (Pittsburgh) has a 2.34 ERA. Steve Carlton (Philadelphia) records the most wins (23). Rollie Fingers (San Diego) has 35 saves. Phil Niekro (Atlanta) fans 262.

NL Batting & Base Running Leaders
Dave Parker (Pittsburgh) wins the NL batting championship (.338) and has the most hits (215). George Foster (Cincinnati) slams 52 homers. Frank Taveras (Pittsburgh) is the base-stealing champ (70). Lou Brock (St. Louis) sets a new NL record for career stolen bases (893).

REGULAR SEASON

American League
AL East The New York Yankees (100-63) win their 3d straight division championship after defeating Boston in a 1-game playoff. Ron Guidry (25-3), Ed Figueroa (20-9) and reliever Goose Gossage (27 saves) head the AL's best pitching staff (3.18 ERA). Reggie Jackson (27 HRs, 97 RBI) and Graig Nettles (27 HRs, 93 RBI) keep the offense rolling.
AL West Kansas City (92-70) repeats as titleholders. Dennis Leonard (21-17), Paul Splitorff (19-13), Larry Gura (16-4) and reliever Al Hrabosky (20 saves) form a solid mound staff. Amos Otis (.298, 22 HRs, 96 RBI) leads the Royal offense.

National League
NL East Philadelphia (90-72) picks up its 3d straight title. Steve Carlton (16-13), Dick Ruthven (13-5) and reliever Ron Reed (17 saves) are the Phillies' top hurlers. Greg Luzinski drives in 101 runs and smacks 35 homers to lead the attack.
NL West Los Angeles (95-67) retains its championship behind a veteran pitching staff featuring Don Sutton (15-11), Burt Hooton (19-10), Tommy John (17-10) and relief ace Terry Forster (22 saves). The offense stars Steve Garvey (.316, 21 HRs, 113 RBI) and Ron Cey (23 HRs, 84 RBI).

ALL-STAR GAME & POSTSEASON GAMES

All-Star Game (San Diego, NL)
The NL scores 4 runs off New York's ace reliever Goose Gossage in the 8th inning to win its 7th straight, 7-3.

AL Championship Series
New York beats Kansas City, 3 games to 1, as Reggie "Mr. October" Jackson hits .462 with 6 RBI and 2 home runs. Ron Guidry, Jim Beattie and Goose Gossage (in relief) pick up the wins.

NL Championship Series
Los Angeles defeats Philadelphia, 3 games to 1. The Dodgers' ace, Tommy John, hurls a 4-hit shutout and relievers Bob Welch and Terry Forster pick up a save each. Steve Garvey (.389, 4 HRs, 7 RBI) and Davey Lopes (.389, 2 HRs, 5 RBI) swing the hot bats for L.A.

World Series
After losing the first 2 games, New York rallies for 4 straight wins over Los Angeles to become world champions for the 22nd time. Bucky Dent (.417, 7 RBI) is a surprise hitting star for New York, teaming up with veteran Reggie Jackson (.391, 2 HRs, 8 RBI) to lead the Yankees. Bill Russell (.423) and Davey Lopes (.308, 3 HRs, 7 RBI) are the leading Dodger hitters.

The remarkable pitching of ace **Ron Guidry** (25–3, 1.74 ERA) leads the New York Yankees to a World Series championship. © National Baseball Library

AWARDS & HONORS

Hall of Fame Inductees
Addie Joss, Eddie Mathews

Most Valuable Players
AL: Jim Rice (Boston)
NL: Dave Parker (Pittsburgh)

Rookies of the Year
AL: Lou Whitaker (Detroit)
NL: Bob Horner (Atlanta)

Cy Young Award Winners
AL: Ron Guidry (New York)
NL: Gaylord Perry (San Diego)

AL Pitching Leaders
Ron Guidry (New York) registers a 1.74 ERA and wins 25 (including 9 shutouts) to lead the AL. Nolan Ryan (California) fans 260. Goose Gossage (New York) saves 27 games.

AL Batting & Base Running Leaders
Jim Rice (Boston) leads in home runs (46), RBI (139) and hits (213). Rod Carew (Minnesota) hits .333 for his 7th batting title. Ron LeFlore (Detroit) wins his first base-stealing crown (68).

NL Pitching Leaders
Craig Swan (New York) has the best ERA (2.43). Gaylord Perry (San Diego) wins 21 games. J. R. Richard (Houston) leads in strikeouts (303). Rollie Fingers (San Diego) registers 37 saves. Bob Forsch (St. Louis) and Tom Seaver (now with Cincinnati) toss no-hitters.

NL Batting & Base Running Leaders
Dave Parker (Pittsburgh) wins the NL batting title (.334). Teammate Omar Moreno steals 71 bases. George Foster (Cincinnati) clouts 40 home runs and drives in 120.

REGULAR SEASON

American League
AL East The Baltimore Orioles (102-57) win their 6th division title. Mike Flanagan (23-9) and relief ace Don Stanhouse (21 saves) are the Orioles' mound stars. Eddie Murray (.295, 25 HRs, 99 RBI) and Ken Singleton (.295, 35 HRs, 111 RBI) lead the team on offense.

AL West California (88-74) picks up its first division title. Don Baylor (.296, 36 HRs, 139 RBI), Bobby Grich (.294, 30 HRs, 101 RBI), Rod Carew (.318) and Dan Ford (.290, 21 HRs, 101 RBI) carry the Angel offense. Dave Frost (16-10), Nolan Ryan (16-14) and Mark Clear (11-5, 14 saves) lead the pitching staff.

National League
NL East Pittsburgh (98-64) captures its 6th title backed by the slugging of Dave Parker (.310, 25 HRs, 94 RBI), Willie Stargell (32 HRs, 82 RBI) and Bill Madlock (.328). On the mound, Kent Tekulve registers 31 saves in 94 appearances. Bert Blyleven (12-5), John Candelaria (14-9) and Bruce Kison (13-7) are winning starters.

NL West Cincinnati finishes on top for the 6th time. Tom Seaver (16-6) and Mike LaCoss (14-8) are the Reds' top pitchers. George Foster (.302, 30 HRs, 98 RBI) is the #1 power hitter.

In his 18th year with the Pittsburgh Pirates, Hall of Famer **Willie Stargell** blasts 3 homers with 8 RBI to lead his team to victory over Baltimore in the 1979 World Series. © National-al Baseball Library

ALL-STAR GAME & POSTSEASON GAMES

All-Star Game (Seattle, AL)
The NL shoves single runs across in the 8th and 9th innings to win its 8th straight over the AL, 7-6. Lee Mazzilli (New York) homers and also scores the winning run.

AL Championship Series
Baltimore defeats California, 3 games to 1. Eddie Murray (.417, 5 RBI) and Pat Kelly (.364, 4 RBI) are the offensive stars. California wildness (18 walks) and failure to hit with men on base prove decisive. Scott McGregor throws a 6-hit shutout to clinch the Series for Baltimore.

NL Championship Series
Pittsburgh sweeps Cincinnati, 3 games to 0. Willie Stargell (.435, 6 RBI) and Phil Garner (.417) star at the plate. Pirate pitchers, led by Bert Blyleven, John Candelaria and Jim Bibby, allow only 5 earned runs in 30 innings.

World Series
Pittsburgh wins the last 3 games to beat Baltimore, 4 games to 3. The Pirates collect 81 hits and compile a .323 team average as the Orioles' relief pitching falters. Willie Stargell (.400, 3 HRs, 7 RBI), Phil Garner (.500, 5 RBI) and Dave Parker (.345) lead the Pirate attack. Kent Tekulve is credited with 3 saves for Pittsburgh.

AWARDS & HONORS

Hall of Fame Inductees
Chuck Klein, Willie Mays, Hack Wilson

Most Valuable Players
AL: Don Baylor (California)
NL: Keith Hernandez (St. Louis)
Willie Stargell (Pittsburgh)

Rookies of the Year
AL: Alfredo Griffin (Toronto) and John Castino (Minnesota)
NL: Rick Sutcliffe (Los Angeles)

Cy Young Award Winners
AL: Mike Flanagan (Baltimore)
NL: Bruce Sutter (Chicago)

AL Pitching Leaders
Ron Guidry (New York) has the best ERA (2.78). Nolan Ryan (California) leads in strikeouts (223). Mike Flanagan (Baltimore) picks up the most wins (23) and Mike Marshall (Minnesota) saves 32 games.

AL Batting & Base Running Leaders
Fred Lynn (Boston) bats .333. Don Baylor (California) knocks in 139 runs and Gorman Thomas (Milwaukee) smashes 45 homers. Willie Wilson (Kansas City) steals 83 bases.

NL Pitching Leaders
J. R. Richard (Houston) is tops in ERA (2.71) and strikeouts (213). Joe Niekro (Houston) and brother Phil Niekro (Atlanta) tie for the most wins (21). Bruce Sutter (Chicago) is credited with 37 saves.

NL Batting & Base Running Leaders
Dave Kingman (Chicago) crushes 48 home runs. Dave Winfield (San Diego) drives home 118 runs. Keith Hernandez (St. Louis) wins the batting title (.344). Omar Moreno (Pittsburgh) repeats as stolen-base champ (77). Lou Brock (St. Louis) steals the 938th base of his career for a new major league record.

1980

REGULAR SEASON

American League
AL East The New York Yankees (103-59) win their 4th title in the last 5 years. Tommy John (22-9), Ron Guidry (17-10) and relief man Goose Gossage (33 saves) lead the mound corps. Reggie Jackson (.300, 41 HRs, 111 RBI) is the team's leading slugger.

AL West Kansas City (97-65) also takes its 4th division title in the last 5 years. Dennis Leonard (20-11), Larry Gura (18-10) and reliever Dan Quisenberry (33 saves) head the pitching staff. George Brett (.390, 24 HRs, 118 RBI), Willie Aikens (20 HRs, 98 RBI) and Willie Wilson (.326, 79 SBs) supply speed and power.

National League
NL East Philadelphia (91-71) wins its 4th title in the last 5 years. Steve Carlton (24-9), Dick Ruthven (17-10) and reliever Tug McGraw (20 saves) are Philadelphia's top moundsmen. Mike Schmidt (48 HRs, 121 RBI) and Bake McBride (.309, 87 RBI) lead the Philly offense.

NL West Houston (93-70) ties Los Angeles for the division title and wins it in a one-game playoff. Joe Niekro (20-12) is the main workhorse on the Astro staff. Jose Cruz (.302, 91 RBI) and Cesar Cedeno (.309, 73 RBI) are Houston's leading hitters.

ALL-STAR GAME & POSTSEASON GAMES

All-Star Game (Los Angeles, NL)
The NL wins its 17th game in the last 18, 4-2. Ken Griffey (Cincinnati) leads the way with a homer and an RBI-single.

AL Championship Series
Kansas City sweeps New York, 3 games to 0, for its first pennant. The Royals' pitching staff limits New York to 5 earned runs. George Brett and Willie Wilson each knock in 4 runs to lead the Kansas City offense.

NL Championship Series
Philadelphia downs Houston, 3 games to 2, for its first flag since 1950. Pete Rose (.400) and Manny Trillo (.381, 4 RBI) lead the Philly attack. Terry Puhl (.526) and Jose Cruz (.400) are Houston's chief run producers.

World Series
The Philadelphia Phillies win their first World Series ever, defeating Kansas City, 4 games to 2. The Philly mound stars are Steve Carlton (2-0) and Tug McGraw (1-1, 2 saves). Mike Schmidt (.381, 2 HRs, 7 RBI), Larry Bowa (.375), Bake McBride (.304, 5 RBI) and Bob Boone (.412, 4 RBI) pace the Philly offense. Amos Otis (.478, 3 HRs, 7 RBI) and Willie Aikens (.400, 4 HRs, 8 RBI) are the hitting stars for Kansas City.

In his second year with Philadelphia, **Pete Rose** and his characteristic hustle spark the Phillies to their first World Series championship. © Bob Bartoss

AWARDS & HONORS

Hall of Fame Inductees
Al Kaline, Duke Snider

Most Valuable Players
AL: George Brett (Kansas City)
NL: Mike Schmidt (Philadelphia)

Rookies of the Year
AL: Joe Charboneau (Cleveland)
NL: Steve Howe (Los Angeles)

Cy Young Award Winners
AL: Steve Stone (Baltimore)
NL: Steve Carlton (Philadelphia)

AL Pitching Leaders
Steve Stone (Baltimore) wins 25 games. Rudy May (New York) is tops in ERA (2.47). Len Barker (Cleveland) leads in strikeouts with 187. Dan Quisenberry (Kansas City) takes over as #1 game saver (33).

AL Batting & Base Running Leaders
George Brett (Kansas City) wins the batting title with ease (.390). Reggie Jackson (New York) and Ben Oglivie (Milwaukee) tie for most home runs (41). Cecil Cooper (Milwaukee) drives in 122 runs. Rickey Henderson (Oakland) steals 100 bases.

NL Pitching Leaders
Steve Carlton (Philadelphia) has the most wins (24) and strikeouts (286). Don Sutton's (Los Angeles) ERA (2.12) leads the NL. Bruce Sutter (Chicago) repeats as the top reliever (28 saves).

NL Batting & Base Running Leaders
Mike Schmidt (Philadelphia) clouts 48 homers and drives in 121 runs to lead the NL. Bill Buckner (Chicago) wins his first batting championship (.324). Ron LeFlore (Montreal) steals 97 bases, 1 more than Omar Moreno of Pittsburgh.

1981

REGULAR SEASON

[Note: Because of a 10-week players' strike, the 1981 season is divided into 2 halves, with the winners of each half meeting in a playoff to determine who goes into the Championship Series.]

American League
AL East The New York Yankees (59-48) win the playoff games against Milwaukee (3 to 2) to capture the division. Ron Guidry (11-5) and relief ace Goose Gossage (20 saves) are the top hurlers. Dave Winfield (13 HRs, 68 RBI) leads the offense.
AL West Oakland (64-45) takes the division, defeating Kansas City, 3 games to 0. Steve McCatty (14-7) is the ace of the pitching staff. Tony Armas (22 HRs, 76 RBI) is the top hitter.

National League
NL East Montreal (60-48) wins the title, defeating Philadelphia, 3 games to 2, in the playoff. Steve Rogers (12-8) is the #1 starter and Andre Dawson (24 HRs, 64 RBI) is the heavy hitter.
NL West Los Angeles comes out on top after beating Houston in the playoff, 3 games to 2. Jerry Reuss (10-4) and Fernando Valenzuela (13-7) are the pitching aces. Ron Cey (13 HRs, 50 RBI), Steve Garvey (10 HRs, 64 RBI), Pedro Guerrero (.300, 12 HRs, 48 RBI) and Dusty Baker (.320, 9 HRs, 49 RBI) run the Dodger offense.

ALL-STAR GAME & POSTSEASON GAMES

All-Star Game (Cleveland, AL)
The NL wins again, 5-4. Home runs by Montreal's Gary Carter (2), Dave Parker (Pittsburgh) and Mike Schmidt (Philadelphia) bury the AL before the largest All-Star crowd ever (72,086).

AL Championship Series
New York beats Oakland, 3 games to 0. Yankee infielder Graig Nettles (.500, 9 RBI) is a one-man wrecking crew. The Yankee pitching squad, led by Tommy John and Dave Righetti, limits Oakland to only 4 earned runs.

NL Championship Series
Los Angeles beats Montreal, 3 games to 2. Burt Hooton (2-0) allows no earned runs in 14⅔ innings to lead the Dodger staff. Rick Monday's 2-out homer in the 9th inning of game 5 wins the game and the pennant for L.A.

World Series
The Los Angeles Dodgers beat the New York Yankees, 4 games to 2, for their first world championship since 1965. Pedro Guerrero (.333, 7 RBI) and Ron Cey (.350, 3 HRs, 6 RBI) are the leading Dodger hitters. Bob Watson (.319, 7 RBI) stars for the Yankees in a losing cause. Pitchers Jerry Reuss, Burt Hooton, Fernando Valenzuela and Steve Howe each win a game for the Dodgers

AWARDS & HONORS

Hall of Fame Inductees
Bob Gibson, Johnny Mize

Most Valuable Players
AL: Rollie Fingers (Milwaukee)
NL: Mike Schmidt (Philadelphia)

Rookies of the Year
AL: Dave Righetti (New York)
NL: Fernando Valenzuela (L.A.)

Cy Young Award Winners
AL: Rollie Fingers (Milwaukee)
NL: Fernando Valenzuela (L.A.)

AL Pitching Leaders
Steve McCatty (Oakland) has the best ERA (2.32) and ties 3 other pitchers with 14 wins. Len Barker (Cleveland) strikes out 127 and pitches a perfect game. Rollie Fingers earns 28 saves.

AL Batting & Base Running Leaders
Eddie Murray (Baltimore) has 78 RBI and ties 3 others with 22 homers. Carney Lansford (Boston) is the batting champion (.336). Rickey Henderson (Oakland) steals 56 bases.

NL Pitching Leaders
Tom Seaver (Cincinnati) leads with 14 wins. Rookie Fernando Valenzuela (Los Angeles) strikes out 180 and tosses 8 shutouts. Nolan Ryan (Houston) earns the lowest ERA (1.69) and hurls his 5th no-hitter, a major league record. Bruce Sutter (St. Louis) leads in games saved (25). Charlie Lea (Montreal) also twirls a no-hitter.

NL Batting & Base Running Leaders
Mike Schmidt (Philadelphia) leads the NL with 31 home runs and 91 RBI. Bill Madlock (Pittsburgh) wins the batting crown (.341) for the 3d time. Tim Raines (Montreal) is the top base stealer (71).

REGULAR SEASON

American League
AL East The Milwaukee Brewers (95-67) win their 1st division title. Pete Vuckovich (18-6), Mike Caldwell (17-13) and reliever Rollie Fingers (29 saves) are the top pitchers. Robin Yount (.331, 29 HRs, 114 RBI), Cecil Cooper (.313, 32 HRs, 121 RBI), Gorman Thomas (39 HRs, 112 RBI) and Ben Oglivie (34 HRs, 102 RBI) power a potent offense (216 HRs).
AL West California (93-69) wins its 2d title behind the power hitting of Reggie Jackson (39 HRs, 101 RBI), Fred Lynn (.299, 21 HRs, 86 RBI), Doug DeCinces (.301, 30 HRs, 97 RBI) and Brian Downing (24 HRs, 84 RBI). Geoff Zahn (18-8) leads the pitching staff.

National League
NL East St. Louis (92-70) wins its first division title. Relief ace Bruce Sutter (36 saves), Joaquin Andujar (15-10) and Bob Forsch (15-9) star on the mound. Keith Hernandez (.299, 94 RBI) and George Hendrick (19 HRs, 104 RBI) lead the Cardinal hitters.
NL West The Atlanta Braves (89-73) win the division for the 1st time since 1969. Phil Niekro, now in his 19th year in the majors, has a 17-4 record. Gene Garber is credited with 30 saves. Dale Murphy (36 HRs, 109 RBI) and Bob Horner (32 HRs, 97 RBI) are the big run producers.

ALL-STAR GAME & POSTSEASON GAMES

All-Star Game (Montreal, NL)
In the first All-Star game played outside the U.S., Dave Concepcion (Cincinnati) homers to lead the NL to its 11th straight win, 4-1.

AL Championship Series
California won the first 2 games, but Milwaukee took the next 3 straight to win the pennant. Paul Molitor (5 RBI) is the Brewers' hitting star. California's Don Baylor (10 RBI) and Fred Lynn (.611) lead all hitters.

NL Championship Series
The St. Louis Cardinals defeat Atlanta, 3 games to 0. The Cardinal pitching staff allows only 5 earned runs and 15 hits. Willie McGee (.308, 5 RBI) leads the offense.

World Series
The St. Louis Cardinals win their first World Series since 1967, beating Milwaukee 4 games to 3 in a thriller. Joaquin Andujar (2-0) and Bruce Sutter (1-0, 2 saves) are the stars of the Cardinal staff. Keith Hernandez (8 RBI) is the leading run producer. Mike Caldwell (2-0) is Milwaukee's mound ace. The Brewers' Robin Yount (.414, 6 RBI) collects 4 hits in 2 Series games, a new record. Paul Molitor's record 5 hits in a Series game (game 1) goes for naught.

AWARDS & HONORS

Hall of Fame Inductees
Hank Aaron, Travis Jackson, Frank Robinson

Most Valuable Players
AL: Robin Yount (Milwaukee)
NL: Dale Murphy (Atlanta)

Rookies of the Year
AL: Cal Ripken (Baltimore)
NL: Steve Sax (Los Angeles)

Cy Young Award Winners
AL: Pete Vuckovich (Milwaukee)
NL: Steve Carlton (Philadelphia)
[Note: Carlton is the only man to win the Cy Young Award 4 times.]

AL Pitching Leaders
Rick Sutcliffe (Cleveland) has the lowest ERA (2.96). Dan Quisenberry (Kansas City) registers 35 saves. Floyd Bannister (Seattle) fans 209, and LaMarr Hoyt (Chicago) wins 19.

AL Batting & Base Running Leaders
Willie Wilson (Kansas City) leads the AL with a .332 average. Reggie Jackson (California) and Gorman Thomas (Milwaukee) stroke 39 homers each. Hal McRae (Kansas City) has 133 RBI. Rickey Henderson (Oakland) steals 130 bases to set a new single-season record.

NL Pitching Leaders
Steve Carlton (Philadelphia), in his 18th year, racks up 23 wins (including 6 shutouts) and 286 strikeouts. Bruce Sutter (St. Louis) turns in 36 saves. Steve Rogers (Montreal) leads the NL with a 2.40 ERA.

NL Batting & Base Running Leaders
Al Oliver (Montreal) drives home 109 runs (tied with Dale Murphy of Atlanta) and hits for a .331 average. Dave Kingman (New York) slams 37 home runs. Tim Raines (Montreal) steals 78 bases.

Rickey Henderson of the Oakland Athletics steals his 119th base of the season to break Lou Brock's record. © National Baseball Library

1983

REGULAR SEASON

American League
AL East Baltimore (98-64) wins the division for the 7th time. Scott McGregor (18-7), Mike Boddicker (16-8) and Mike Flanagan (12-4) head a strong pitching staff. Eddie Murray (.306, 33 HRs, 111 RBI) and Cal Ripken (.318, 27 HRs, 102 RBI) lead the Oriole offense (168 HRs).
AL West Chicago (99-63) wins its division for the first time. LaMarr Hoyt (24-10) and Rich Dotson (22-7) lead a strong mound corps. Rookie Ron Kittle (35 HRs, 100 RBI), Harold Baines (20 HRs, 99 RBI) and Carlton Fisk (26 HRs, 86 RBI) are Chicago's leading hitters.

National League
NL East Philadelphia (90-72) takes its 5th division title. John Denny (19-6), Ron Reed (9-1) and relief ace Al Holland (25 saves) are the pitching stars. Mike Schmidt (40 HRs, 109 RBI) carries the offensive load.
NL West Los Angeles (91-71) also takes its 5th division championship. No Dodger pitcher wins more than 15 games, but Steve Howe, Dave Stewart and Tom Niedenfuer combine for 17 wins and 37 saves. Pedro Guerrero (.298, 32 HRs, 103 RBI) is the heavy hitter in a lineup that bats only .250.

ALL-STAR GAME & POSTSEASON GAMES

All-Star Game (Chicago, AL)
On the 50th anniversary of the All-Star game, the AL breaks the NL's 11-game winning streak with a 13-3 trouncing. A 3rd-inning grand slam—the first in an All-Star game—by California's Fred Lynn is the clincher.

AL Championship Series
Baltimore wins its 6th pennant, beating Chicago 3 games to 1. The Oriole pitching staff allows only 2 earned runs in 37 innings. Eddie Murray, Cal Ripken and Gary Roenicke score a combined 14 runs.

NL Championship Series
Philadelphia wins its 2d pennant, defeating Los Angeles 3 games to 1. Steve Carlton (2-0) is the pitching star for the Phillies. Gary Matthews (.429, 3 HRs, 8 RBI) pace the Philadelphia offense.

World Series
Led by its brilliant pitching staff, Baltimore defeats Philadelphia, 4 games to 1, for its 3d world championship. The Phillies score only 9 runs in 5 games as Baltimore pitchers have a combined ERA of 1.60. Rick Dempsey (4 doubles and a homer) is the Orioles' hitting hero. Joe Morgan blasts 2 home runs for the losing Phillies.

AWARDS & HONORS

Hall of Fame Inductees
Walter Alston, George Kell, Juan Marichal, Brooks Robinson

Most Valuable Players
AL: Cal Ripken (Baltimore)
NL: Dale Murphy (Atlanta)

Rookies of the Year
AL: Ron Kittle (Chicago)
NL: Darryl Strawberry (New York)

Cy Young Award Winners
AL: LaMarr Hoyt (Chicago)
NL: John Denny (Philadelphia)

AL Pitching Leaders
Rick Honeycutt (Texas) has the best ERA (2.42). LaMarr Hoyt (Chicago) picks up the most wins (24). Dan Quisenberry (Kansas City) is credited with 45 saves (a new AL record). Jack Morris (Detroit) strikes out 232.

AL Batting & Base Running Leaders
Wade Boggs (Boston) wins his first batting championship (.361). Teammate Jim Rice is the home-run king (39). He also ties Cecil Cooper for most RBI (126). Rickey Henderson (Oakland) has 108 stolen bases.

NL Pitching Leaders
John Denny (Philadelphia) wins 19 games, and teammate Steve Carlton strikes out 275. Atlee Hammaker (San Francisco) has the lowest ERA (2.25). Lee Smith (Chicago) is the NL's top reliever (29 saves). Bob Forsch (St. Louis) pitches his 2d no-hitter.

NL Batting & Base Running Leaders
Mike Schmidt (Philadelphia) belts 40 homers. Bill Madlock (Pittsburgh) wins the NL batting title (.323). Atlanta's Dale Murphy drives in 121 runs. Tim Raines (Montreal) steals 90 bases for his 3d straight title.

1984

REGULAR SEASON

American League
AL East The Detroit Tigers (104-58) win their 2d division title (and first since 1972). A strong pitching staff is led by Jack Morris (19-11), Dan Petry (18-8), Milt Wilcox (17-8) and reliever Willie Hernandez (32 saves). **AL West** Kansas City (84-78) captures its 6th title. Dan Quisenberry's relief pitching (44 saves) is a major factor. Steve Balboni (28 HRs, 77 RBI) is the Royals' top slugger

National League
NL East The Chicago Cubs (96-65) win the division for the first time. Rick Sutcliffe's 16-1 record is the best in the majors. Lee Smith (33 saves) is a major contributor. Ron Cey (25 HRs, 97 RBI), Leon "Bull" Durham (23 HRs, 96 RBI), Jody Davis (19 HRs, 94 RBI) and Ryne Sandberg (.314, 19 HRs, 84 RBI) spark the Cubs' potent offense. **NL West** San Diego (92-70) also is a first-time winner. The only pitcher on the staff with 15 wins is Eric Show (15-9), but Goose Gossage (25 saves) and Craig Lefferts (10 saves) rescue the Padres. Tony Gwynn (.351), Kevin McReynolds (20 HRs, 75 RBI) and Steve Garvey (.284, 8 HRs, 86 RBI) produce the runs.

ALL-STAR GAME & POSTSEASON GAMES

All-Star Game (San Francisco, NL)
Dwight Gooden (New York), 19, the youngest player ever to appear in an All-Star game, and Fernando Valenzuela (Los Angeles), 23, strike out 6 consecutive AL hitters to lead the NL to victory, 3-1. Gary Carter (Montreal) and Dale Murphy (Atlanta) belt home runs for the NL.

AL Championship Series
Detroit sweeps Kansas City, 3 games to 0. The Tiger pitching staff, led by Milt Wilcox, Jack Morris and Dan Petry, holds the Royals to 4 runs and only 2 extra base hits. Alan Trammell (.364) and Kirk Gibson (.417) lead Detroit's offense.

NL Championship Series
San Diego defeats Chicago, 3 games to 2. Steve Garvey (.400, 7 RBI) leads the Padres' hitting attack. Reliever Craig Lefferts gets credit for 2 wins. Jody Davis (.389, 2 HRs, 6 RBI) is the hitting star for Chicago.

World Series
Detroit captures its 4th world championship, defeating San Diego 4 games to 1. Detroit's manager, Sparky Anderson, is the first man to manage a World Series winner in both leagues. Alan Trammell (.450, 2 HRs, 6 RBI) and Kirk Gibson (.333, 2 HRs, 7 RBI) take charge of the Tiger offense. In game 3, 3 San Diego pitchers walk 11 men and both teams leave 24 men on base, setting new Series records.

AWARDS & HONORS

Hall of Fame Inductees
Luis Aparicio, Don Drysdale, Rick Ferrell, Harmon Killebrew, Pee Wee Reese

Most Valuable Players
AL: Willie Hernandez (Detroit)
NL: Ryne Sandberg (Chicago)

Rookies of the Year
AL: Alvin Davis (Seattle)
NL: Dwight Gooden (New York)

Cy Young Award Winners
AL: Willie Hernandez (Detroit)
NL: Rick Sutcliffe (Chicago)

AL Pitching Leaders
Mike Boddicker (Baltimore) wins the most games (20) and has the lowest ERA (2.79). Dan Quisenberry (Kansas City) saves 44 games, and rookie Mark Langston (Seattle) registers the most strikeouts (204).

AL Batting & Base Running Leaders
Don Mattingly (New York) bats .343 and collects 207 hits. Tony Armas (Boston) slams 43 home runs and drives in 123 runs. Rickey Henderson (Oakland) leads in stolen bases (66) for the 5th year in a row.

NL Pitching Leaders
Joaquin Andujar (St. Louis) has the most wins (20). Teammate Bruce Sutter gets 45 saves (tying Dan Quisenberry's major league record). Alejandro Pena (Los Angeles) has the best ERA (2.48). Dwight Gooden (New York) fans 276.

NL Batting & Base Running Leaders
Tony Gwynn (San Diego) takes the batting title (.351). Mike Schmidt (Philadelphia) and Dale Murphy (Atlanta) tie for the most home runs (36). Schmidt is also tied by Gary Carter (Montreal) for the most RBI (106). Tim Raines (Montreal) steals the most bases (75).

1985

REGULAR SEASON

American League
AL East The Toronto Blue Jays (99-62) win their first division title. Dennis Lamp (11-0), Doyle Alexander (17-10), Jimmy Key (14-6) and relief men Bill Caudill and Tom Henke (27 saves combined), lead the AL's top pitching staff (3.31 ERA).

AL West Kansas City (91-71) takes its 7th division championship. Bret Saberhagen (20-6) and Charlie Leibrandt (17-9) are the Royals' best starters. Dan Quisenberry (37 saves) remains the AL's top reliever. George Brett (.335, 30 HRs, 112 RBI) and Steve Balboni (36 HRs, 88 RBI) are the heavy hitters.

National League
NL East St. Louis (101-61) wins its 2d division title. John Tudor (21-8), Joaquin Andujar (21-12) and Danny Cox (18-9) are the top starters. Tommy Herr (.302, 110 RBI) and Jack Clark (22 HRs, 87 RBI) lead the Cardinal offense.

NL West Los Angeles (95-67) wins its division for a 6th time behind a strong pitching staff led by Orel Hershiser (19-3), Fernando Valenzuela (17-10) and Bob Welch (14-4). Pedro Guerrero (.320, 33 HRs, 87 RBI) and Mike Marshall (.293, 28 HRs, 95 RBI) supply the power.

New York Met pitcher **Dwight "Doc" Gooden** has a phenomenal season (24–4, 1.53 ERA). At the age of 20 he becomes the youngest pitcher ever to win 20 games and the Cy Young Award. © CSU

ALL-STAR GAME & POSTSEASON GAMES

All-Star Game (Minnesota, AL)
The NL defeats the AL, 6-1, for its 21st win in 23 games. Five NL pitchers hold the AL to only 5 singles.

AL Championship Series
[Note: The Championship Series in both leagues are now "best 4-out-of-7."]
Kansas City downs Toronto, 4 games to 3. George Brett (.348, 3 HRs, 5 RBI) and Jim Sundberg (6 RBI) lead the way on offense. Danny Jackson (1-0) twirls a key shutout (game 5) for the Royals.

NL Championship Series
St. Louis defeats Los Angeles, 4 games to 2. Jack Clark's 3-run homer with 2 out in the 9th inning of game 6 clinches the pennant for the Cardinals. Ozzie Smith (.435) and Tommy Herr (.333, 6 RBI) lead the Cardinal attack.

World Series
Kansas City defeats St. Louis, 4 games to 3, for its first world championship. Bret Saberhagen (2-0) allows only 1 run in 18 innings. Willie Wilson (.367), Frank White (6 RBI) and George Brett (.370) are the heavy hitters for Kansas City. John Tudor (2-1) stars on the mound for St. Louis. Cardinal rookie reliever Todd Worrell fans 6 in a row (game 5) to tie the Series record.

AWARDS & HONORS

Hall of Fame Inductees
Lou Brock, Enos Slaughter, Arky Vaughan, Hoyt Wilhelm

Most Valuable Players
AL: Don Mattingly (New York)
NL: Willie McGee (St. Louis)

Rookies of the Year
AL: Ozzie Guillen (Chicago)
NL: Vince Coleman (St. Louis)

Cy Young Award Winners
AL: Bret Saberhagen (Kansas City)
NL: Dwight Gooden (New York)

AL Pitching Leaders
Ron Guidry (New York) posts the most wins (22). Dave Stieb (Toronto) has the lowest ERA (2.48). Dan Quisenberry (Kansas City) turns in 37 saves. Bert Blyleven (Cleveland/Minnesota) leads in strikeouts (206).

AL Batting & Base Running Leaders
Don Mattingly (New York) has the most RBI (145). Wade Boggs (Boston) leads the AL in batting (.368), and Darrell Evans (Detroit) smacks 40 homers. Rickey Henderson (New York) steals 80 bases.

NL Pitching Leaders
Dwight Gooden (New York) has the lowest ERA (1.53), the most wins (24) and the most strikeouts (268). Jeff Reardon (Montreal) is the #1 game saver (41).

NL Batting & Base Running Leaders
Willie McGee (St. Louis) wins the batting championship (.353) and collects the most hits (216). Dale Murphy (Atlanta) clouts 37 home runs and Dave Parker (Cincinnati) drives in 125 runs. Rookie Vince Coleman (St. Louis) steals 110 bases. Pete Rose (Cincinnati) gets hit #4,192 to surpass Ty Cobb's 57-year-old record for hits in a career.

REGULAR SEASON

American League

AL East The Boston Red Sox (95-66) win their 2d division title. Roger Clemens (24-4, 2.48 ERA) is the ace of the Red Sox pitching staff. Jim Rice (.324, 20 HRs, 110 RBI), Dwight Evans (26 HRs, 97 RBI), Bill Buckner (102 RBI) and Don Baylor (31 HRs, 94 RBI) are the batting stars. **AL West** California captures its 3d title behind the pitching of Mike Witt (18-10), John Candelaria (10-2), Kirk McCaskill (17-10) and reliever Donnie Moore (21 saves). Wally Joyner (22 HRs, 100 RBI), Doug DeCinces (26 HRs, 96 RBI) and Brian Downing (20 HRs, 95 RBI) produce the runs.

National League

NL East The New York Mets (108-54) win the division for the 3d time behind solid pitching (6 finish with 10 or more wins). Relievers Roger McDowell and Jesse Orosco combine for 43 saves. Gary Carter (24 HRs, 105 RBI), Darryl Strawberry (27 HRs, 93 RBI) and Keith Hernandez (.310, 83 RBI) lead the Mets' attack. **NL West** Houston (96-66) finishes on top for the 3d time, with 5 pitchers winning 10 or more games. Relief ace Dave Smith has 33 saves. Glenn Davis (31 HRs, 101 RBI) and Kevin Bass (.311, 20 HRs, 79 RBI) are the offensive stars.

The MVP right fielder for the Oakland Athletics, **Jose Canseco** becomes the first player in baseball history to hit 40 home runs and steal 40 bases in the same season.

ALL-STAR GAME & POSTSEASON GAMES

All-Star Game (Houston, NL)

The AL breaks through with a rare victory, 3-2. Lou Whitaker's (Detroit) homer in the 2d inning spells the difference. Fernando Valenzuela (Los Angeles) fans 5 in a row for the NL.

AL Championship Series

Boston wins an exciting 7-game Series over California, 4 games to 3. Marty Barrett (.367, 5 RBI), Jim Rice (2 HRs, 6 RBI) and Rich Gedman (.357, 6 RBI) lead the Boston attack. Bob Boone (.455) and Brian Downing (7 RBI) star at bat for the Angels.

NL Championship Series

New York defeats Houston, 4 games to 2, taking the final game, 7-6, in a 16-inning thriller. The Mets' relief ace, Jesse Orosco, gets credit for 3 wins in only 8 innings pitched. Darryl Strawberry drives in 5 runs with 2 homers and a double. Mike Scott (2-0, 19 strikeouts, 0.50 ERA) shines for the Astros.

World Series

The New York Mets win their 2d world championship in a dramatic 7-game Series against the Boston Red Sox. Ray Knight (.391, 5 RBI), Gary Carter (2 HRs, 9 RBI) and Lenny Dykstra (.296, 2 HRs) lead the Mets' hit parade. Ron Darling (1-1), Bob Ojeda (1-0) and Jesse Orosco (2 saves) allow a combined 6 earned runs in 36⅔ innings. Dave Henderson (.400, 2 HRs), Marty Barrett (.433) and Dwight Evans (2 HRs, 9 RBI) are Boston's top run producers. Bruce Hurst wins 2 games for the Red Sox. In the exciting finale (game 7), 10 pitchers see action. The Mets win by scoring 8 runs in the last 3 innings as Boston drops its 4th 7-game Series since 1918.

AWARDS & HONORS

Hall of Fame Inductees

Bobby Doerr, Ernie Lombardi, Willie McCovey

Most Valuable Players

AL: Roger Clemens (Boston)
NL: Mike Schmidt (Philadelphia)

Rookies of the Year

AL: Jose Canseco (Oakland)
NL: Todd Worrell (St. Louis)

Cy Young Award Winners

AL: Roger Clemens (Boston)
NL: Mike Scott (Houston)

AL Pitching Leaders

Roger Clemens (Boston) has 24 wins and a 2.48 ERA. Dave Righetti (New York) picks up 46 saves, a new major league record. Mark Langston (Seattle) is the strikeout king (245). Joe Cowley (Chicago) hurls a no-hitter.

AL Batting & Base Running Leaders

Wade Boggs (Boston) wins his 3d batting title (.357). Jesse Barfield (Toronto) belts 40 homers, and Joe Carter (Cleveland) drives home 121. Rickey Henderson (New York) wins his 7th straight base-stealing crown (87).

NL Pitching Leaders

Fernando Valenzuela (Los Angeles) has 21 wins and 20 complete games. Mike Scott (Houston) strikes out 306, has the best ERA (2.22) and tosses a no-hitter. Todd Worrell (St. Louis) picks up 36 saves to lead the league.

NL Batting & Base Running Leaders

Mike Schmidt (Philadelphia) leads the NL in home runs (37) for the 8th time, and in RBI (119) for the 4th time. Tim Raines (Montreal) is the leading hitter (.334) and Vince Coleman (St. Louis) steals 107 bases to retain his title.

1987

REGULAR SEASON

American League
AL East Detroit (98-64) captures its 3d division crown. Alan Trammell (.343, 28 HRs, 105 RBI), Darrell Evans (34 HRs, 99 RBI) and rookie Matt Nokes (32 HRs, 87 RBI) lead the Tiger offense. Jack Morris (18-11), Frank Tanana (15-10), Doyle Alexander (9-0) and Walt Terrell (17-10) are Detroit's pitching aces. Don Mattingly (New York) hits 6 grand-slam home runs in one season, a new major-league record.
AL West Minnesota (85-77) takes its 3d division title. Frank Viola (17-10) and Jeff Reardon (31 saves) are the mound stars. Gary Gaetti (31 HRs, 109 RBI), Kent Hrbek (34 HRs, 90 RBI) and Kirby Puckett (.332, 28 HRs, 99 RBI) star on offense.

National League
NL East St. Louis (95-67) wins for the 3d time in 6 years behind the heavy hitting of Jack Clark (35 HRs, 106 RBI), Willie McGee (105 RBI) and Terry Pendleton (96 RBI). No Cardinal pitcher produces more than 11 wins. Todd Worrell registers 33 saves.
NL West San Francisco (90-72) wins its 2d title with good pitching (.368 team ERA) and the power hitting of Will Clark (.308, 35 HRs, 91 RBI), Chili Davis (24 HRs, 76 RBI) and Candy Maldonado (20 HRs, 85 RBI).

ALL-STAR GAME & POSTSEASON GAMES

All-Star Game (Oakland, AL)
After a scoreless duel for 12 innings, the NL wins 2-0 in the 13th on Tim Raines' (Montreal) 2-out triple.

AL Championship Series
The Minnesota Twins trounce Detroit, 4 games to 1, for their 2d pennant. Bert Blyleven wins 2 games for the Twins and Tom Brunansky comes through with 9 RBI.

NL Championship Series
St. Louis captures its 15th NL pennant, defeating San Francisco 4 games to 3, despite 9 homers by the Giants (4 by Jeff Leonard). Ken Dayley stars in relief for the Cardinals with 2 saves. Danny Cox hurls a shutout in game 7 to send the Cardinals to the World Series.

World Series
Minnesota wins its first World Series, upsetting St. Louis 4 games to 3. Frank Viola (2-1) and Bert Blyleven (1-1) are the mound heroes for the Twins. Dan Gladden (7 RBI), Steve Lombardozzi (.412) and Kirby Puckett (.357) pace the Minnesota attack. Dan Gladden and Kent Hrbek both hit grand-slam home runs to clinch games 1 and 6 for the Twins. Willie McGee (.370) and Tony Pena (.409) are the leading Cardinal hitters.

AWARDS & HONORS

Hall of Fame Inductees
Catfish Hunter, Billy Williams, Ray Dandridge

Most Valuable Players
AL: George Bell (Toronto)
NL: Andre Dawson (Chicago)

Rookies of the Year
AL: Mark McGwire (Oakland)
NL: Benito Santiago (San Diego)

Cy Young Award Winners
AL: Roger Clemens (Boston)
NL: Steve Bedrosian (Philadelphia)

AL Pitching Leaders
Roger Clemens (Boston) has the most wins (20, tied with Dave Stewart of Oakland), including 7 shutouts. Jimmy Key (Toronto) sports the lowest ERA (2.76). Teammate Tom Henke has 34 saves.

AL Batting & Base Running Leaders
Wade Boggs (Boston) takes his 4th batting crown (.363). Oakland's Mark McGwire hits 49 home runs. George Bell (Toronto) leads in RBI (134). Harold Reynolds (Seattle) is the stolen-base leader (60).

NL Pitching Leaders
Nolan Ryan (Houston) has the most strikeouts (270) for the 8th time in his career (he is now the all-time strikeout king with 4,547). Ryan's ERA (2.76) also leads the NL. Rick Sutcliffe (Chicago) has the most wins (18). Steve Bedrosian (Philadelphia) has 40 saves.

NL Batting & Base Running Leaders
Tony Gwynn (San Diego) wins his 2d batting championship (.370) and collects the most hits (218). Andre Dawson (Chicago) leads in home runs (49) and RBI (137). Vince Coleman (St. Louis) steals 109 bases.

1988

REGULAR SEASON

AMERICAN LEAGUE
AL East The Boston Red Sox (89-73), sparked by Mike Greenwell (.325, 119 RBI), Wade Boggs (.366) and Dwight Evans (111 RBI), win the division. Bruce Hurst (18-6) and Roger Clemens (18-12) lead the pitching staff.
AL West The Oakland Athletics (104-58) beat Minnesota by 13 games. Outfielder Jose Canseco (.307, 124 RBI) is the first "40/40" player (42 home runs and 40 stolen bases). The pitching corps is led by Dave Stewart (21-12), Bob Welch (17-9) and reliever Dennis Eckersley (45 saves).

National League
NL East The New York Mets (100-60) beat out 2d place Pittsburgh by 15 games. Darryl Strawberry (39 HRs, 101 RBI) and Kevin Mc-Reynolds (27 HRs, 99 RBI) carry the heavy bats. The mound corps features David Cone (20-3), Dwight Gooden (18-9) and Ron Darling (17-9).
NL West The Los Angeles Dodgers (94-67) finish first with a solid pitching staff. Orel Hershiser (23-8) hurls a record 59 consecutive scoreless innings. Jay Howell (21 saves) is the relief specialist. Kirk Gibson (.290, 25 HRs) and Mike Marshall (20 HRs, 82 RBI) supply the offensive punch.

Orel Hershiser of the Los Angeles Dodgers makes baseball history, hurling 59 consecutive scoreless innings to break Don Drysdale's record.

ALL-STAR GAME & POSTSEASON GAMES

All-Star Game (Cincinnati, NL)
The AL wins its 2d game in 3 years, 2-0. Terry Steinbach, Oakland A's catcher, leads off the 3d inning with a solo home run, then adds a sacrifice fly in the 4th to account for both AL runs.

AL Championship Series
The Oakland A's completely dominate the Boston Red Sox, sweeping the series 4 games to none. Jose Canseco, Oakland's slugging outfielder, slams 3 home runs in the series and Dennis Eckersley, the A's top reliever, records 4 saves.

NL Championship Series
The Los Angeles Dodgers defeat the heavily favored New York Mets in a dramatic 7-game series. Orel Hershiser, the Dodgers' pitching ace, hurls a shutout in the final game after starting games 1 and 3 and relieving in game 5. Rookie Tim Belcher picks up 2 wins for the Dodgers. Kirk Gibson slams 2 game-winning homers and Mike Scioscia belts a pivotal round-tripper in game 4.

World Series
The Los Angeles Dodgers complete their amazing performance, upsetting the Oakland A's, 4 games to 1, including a 3-game sweep in Oakland's own park. Orel Hershiser and the rest of the Dodger staff handcuff Oakland's sluggers, Jose Canseco and Mark McGwire, with only one hit apiece for the 5-game series. In the opening game, Kirk Gibson, Los Angeles' injured star, caps one of the most dramatic scenes in World Series history, hobbling off the bench and smacking a pinch-hit, game-winning home run in the 9th inning against Oakland's relief ace, Dennis Eckersley. Hershiser—who wins 2 games, strikes out 17, and allows only 2 earned runs in 18 innings—is named the Series MVP.

AWARDS & HONORS

Hall of Fame Inductees
Willie Stargell, Carl Yastrzemski, Johnny Bench

Most Valuable Players
AL: Jose Canseco (Oakland)
NL: Kirk Gibson (Los Angeles)

Rookies of the Year
AL: Walt Weiss (Oakland)
NL: Chris Sabo (Cincinnati)

Cy Young Award Winners
AL: Frank Viola (Minnesota)
NL: Orel Hershiser (Los Angeles)

AL Pitching Leaders
Frank Viola (Minnesota) collects 24 wins. Roger Clemens (Boston) heads the strikeout parade (291). Dennis Eckersley (Oakland) has 45 saves. Allan Anderson (Minnesota) and Ted Higuera (Milwaukee) share ERA honors (2.45).

AL Batting & Base Running Leaders
Wade Boggs (Boston) captures his 5th batting title (.366). Jose Canseco (Oakland) is the AL's top slugger with 124 RBI and 42 HRs. Rickey Henderson (New York) regains the base-stealing title (his 8th) with 93.

NL Pitching Leaders
Orel Hershiser (Los Angeles) and Danny Jackson (Cincinnati) both win 23 games. Joe Magrane (St. Louis) has the best ERA (2.18) and John Franco (Cincinnati) collects the most saves (39). Nolan Ryan (Houston) leads in strikeouts (228) for the 9th time in his 22-year career.

NL Batting & Base Running Leaders
Tony Gwynn (San Diego) wins the batting title (.313). Darryl Strawberry (New York) captures the home-run crown (39) and Will Clark of San Francisco has the most RBI (109). Vince Coleman (St. Louis) takes his 4th straight base-stealing title (81).

INDEX

A

Aaron, Hank 54-58, 61, 64-65, 67, 70, 72, 80
Abbaticchio, Ed 5
Abernathy, Ted 63, 65
Adams, Ace 41-43
Adams, Babe (Charles) 7
Agee, Tommy 64, 67
Aguirre, Hank 60
Aikens, Willie 78
Aker, Jack 64
Aldridge, Vic 23
Alexander, Dale 30
Alexander, Doyle 83, 85
Alexander, Grover Cleveland 9-10, 12-15, 17-18, 24, 26, 36
Allen, Johnny 30, 35
Allen, Richie 62, 70, 72
Allison, Bob 57, 63
Alou, Felipe 60, 66
Alou, Matty 64, 70
Alston, Walter 81
Altrock, Nick 4
Ames, Red (Leon) 7, 12, 14
Anderson, Allan 86
Anderson, John 4
Anderson, Sparky (George Lee) 82
Andujar, Joaquin 80, 82-83
Angels—See California Angels; Los Angeles Angels
Anson, Cap (Adrian) 39
Antonelli, Johnny 52
Aparicio, Luis 54-62, 82
Appling, Luke 34, 41, 62
Arellanes, Frank 7
Armas, Tony 79, 82
Arroyo, Luis 59
Ashburn, Richie 46, 53, 56
Athletics—See Oakland Athletics; Philadelphia Athletics
Atlanta Braves (NL) 80
Auker, Eldon 32-33
Averill, Earl 73
Avila, Bobby 52

B

Bagby, Jim 18
Bahnsen, Stan 66
Baines, Harold 81
Baker, Dusty 75, 79
Baker, Frank 8-12, 53
Balboni, Steve 82-83
Baltimore Orioles (AL) 58, 62, 64, 66-69, 71-72, 77, 81
Bancroft, Dave 69
Bando, Sal 69, 71-72
Banks, Ernie 56-58, 75
Bannister, Floyd 80
Barfield, Jesse 84
Barker, Len 78-79
Barnes, Jesse 17, 19-20
Barnes, Virgil 22
Barney, Rex 46
Barnhart, Clyde 23
Barrett, Johnny 42
Barrett, Marty 84
Barrett, Red (Charles) 43
Bass, Kevin 84
Bauer, Hank 55-56, 8449
Baumann, Frank 58
Bay, Harry 1
Baylor, Don 77, 80, 84
Bearden, Gene 46
Beattie, Jim 76
Beazley, Johnny 40
Beck, Fred 8
Beckley, Jake 69
Bedient, Hugh 10
Bedrosian, Steve 85
Beebe, Fred 4

Belcher, Tim 86
Bell, George 85
Bell, Hi 28
Bell, James (Cool Papa) 72
Bell, Les 24
Bench, Johnny 66, 68, 70-74, 86
Bender, Chief 3, 8-9, 11-12
Bentley, Jack 22
Benton, Al 38-40
Benton, Larry 26
Benton, Rube (John) 13
Benz, Joe 12
Berger, Wally 33
Berra, Yogi (Laurence Peter) 45, 47-56, 62, 70
Bescher, Bob 7, 9-10
Bessent, Don 53
Bibby, Jim 77
Bickford, Vern 46, 48
Billingham, Jack 70-71
Black, Don 45
Black, Joe 50
Black Sox Scandal 17
Blackwell, Ewell 45
Blair, Paul 67-68
Blanchard, Johnny 59
Blanton, Cy 33
Blass, Steve 69-70
Blefary, Curt 63
Blue, Vida (Rochelle) 69, 71-73
Blyleven, Bert 77, 83, 85
Boddicker, Mike 81-82
Boggs, Wade 81, 83-86
Bonds, Bobby 69
Bonham, Ernie 38, 40-41
Boone, Bob 78, 84
Boone, Ray 52
Borowy, Hank 40-41, 43
Bosman, Dick 67, 73
Boston Braves (NL) 12-13, 24, 46
Boston Red Sox (AL) 1-3, 10, 12-16, 36-37, 39, 44, 46-48, 65, 73, 84, 86
Bottomley, Jim 24, 26, 29, 72
Boudreau, Lou 40, 42, 46, 68
Bouton, Jim 61-62
Bowa, Larry 78
Bowman, Bob 37
Boyer, Ken 54, 62
Brain, Dave 5
Branca, Ralph 45, 47
Braves—See Atlanta Braves; Milwaukee Braves
Braxton, Garland 25-26
Brazle, Al 50-51
Brecheen, Harry 42, 44, 46
Bresnahan, Roger 43
Brett, George 74-75, 78, 83
Brewers—See Milwaukee Brewers
Bridges, Marshall 60
Bridges, Tommy 32-34
Briles, Nelson 65-66
Brock, Lou 62, 64-67, 69-71, 77, 83
Broglio, Ernie 58
Brooklyn Dodgers (NL) 14, 38-40, 43-45, 47-54, 56
Brosnan, Jim 59
Brouthers, Dan 43
Brown, Boardwalk 11
Brown, Bobby 47
Brown, Clint 35
Brown, Jimmy 40
Brown, Mace 35
Brown, Mordecai (Three Finger Brown) 4-9, 47
Browns—See St. Louis Browns
Brunansky, Tom 85
Bruton, Bill 51-53, 56
Bryant, Clay 36
Bryant, Ron 71
Buckner, Bill 78, 84
Buhl, Bob 55
Bumbry, Al 71
Bunker, Wally 64
Bunning, Jim 55-58, 65
Burdette, Lew 54-56, 58
Burke, Bob 29

Burkett, Jesse 44
Burns, George (Henry) 24
Burns, George (Joseph) 12, 17, 19
Burroughs, Jeff 72
Bush, Guy 23, 27, 30
Bush, Smoky Joe (Leslie Ambrose) 11-12, 14, 20-21
Byrd, Harry 50
Byrne, Tommy 48, 53

C

Caldwell, Mike 80
Caldwell, Ray 17-18
California Angels (AL) 77, 80, 84
Callison, Johnny 62
Camilli, Dolf 39
Camnitz, Howie 7
Campanella, Roy 47, 49, 50-51, 53, 67
Campaneris, Bert 63-66, 68, 70-72
Campbell, Bill 75
Campbell, Bruce 38
Candelaria, John 75, 77, 84
Canseco, Jose 86
Capra, Buzz (Lee William) 72
Cardinals—See St. Louis Cardinals
Cardwell, Don 58
Carew, Rod 65, 67, 70-73, 75-77
Carey, Max 11, 13-16, 18, 20-24, 59
Carleton, Tex 38
Carlton, Steve 65, 70, 72, 74-76, 78, 80-81
Carroll, Clay 70
Carter, Gary 79, 82, 84
Carter, Joe 84
Carty, Rico 68
Case, George 37-41, 44
Casey, Hugh 40, 45
Cash, Norm 59, 66
Caster, George 42
Castino, John 77
Caudill, Bill 83
Cavarretta, Phil 42-43
Cedeno, Cesar 74, 78
Cepeda, Orlando 56, 59-60, 65, 67
Cey, Ron 72, 75-76, 79, 82
Chambers, Cliff 49
Chambliss, Chris 69, 74-75
Chance, Dean 62
Chance, Frank 1, 4-5, 8, 44
Chandler, Spud (Spurgeon) 36, 40-41, 45
Chapman, Ben 29-31, 35
Charboneau, Joe 78
Charleston, Oscar 74
Chase, Hal 14
Cheney, Larry 10-11, 14
Chesbro, Jack 2, 44
Chicago Cubs (NL) 4-9, 16, 27-28, 30, 33, 36, 43, 68, 82
Chicago White Sox (AL) 3-4, 6, 14-15, 17-18, 55-57, 61-63, 81
Christensen, Larry 75
Christopher, Russ 46
Cicotte, Ed 15, 17
Cincinnati Reds (NL) 17, 24, 37-38, 59, 68, 70-71, 73-74, 77
Clark, Jack 83, 85
Clark, Will 85-865
Clarke, Fred 1, 43
Clarkson, John 61
Clear, Mark 77
Clemens, Roger 84-86
Clemente, Roberto 58-60, 62-65, 68-71
Clendenon, Donn 67
Cleveland Indians (AL) 4, 6, 16-18, 24, 38, 46, 49-54, 56
Coakley, Andy 3
Coates, Jim 58
Cobb, Ty 5-20, 34, 71
Cochrane, Mickey 26-28, 32, 45
Colavito, Rocky 57, 60, 63

Colborn, Jim 75
Cole, King 8
Coleman, Gordy 59
Coleman, Joe H. 70
Coleman, Joe P. 55
Coleman, Vince 83-86
Collins, Eddie 8, 11-12, 15, 17, 21-22, 37
Collins, Jimmy 43
Collins, Phil 31
Collins, Rip (Harry Warner) 32
Combes, Earl 24, 68
Comiskey, Charles 39
Concepcion, Dave 80
Cone, David 86
Conigliaro, Tony 63
Conley, Gene 53
Connolly, Joe 12
Connor, Roger 74
Coombs, Jack 8-9
Cooper, Cecil 78, 80-81
Cooper, Mort 40-42
Cooper, Walker 40-42
Cooper, Wilbur 19
Coveleski, Sam 18, 21, 23, 67
Cowens, Al 75
Cowley, Joe 84
Cox, Danny 83, 85
Craig, Roger 53, 57
Cramer, Doc (Roger Maxwell) 43
Cravath, Gavvy 11-13, 15-16
Crawford, Sam 1, 5-6, 8, 12-13, 55
Cronin, Joe 31-32, 35, 54
Crosetti, Frank 35-36
Crowder, General 30-31, 33
Cruz, Jose 78
Cubs—See Chicago Cubs
Cuellar, Mike 67-69, 72
Cullenbine, Roy 43
Cummings, Candy 39
Cuyler, Kiki 22-28, 66

D

Dahlen, Bill 2
Daley, Buddy 59
Dandridge, Ray 85
Danforth, Dave 15
Dark, Alvin 46, 49, 52
Darling, Ron 84, 86
Daubert, Jake 11-12
Davies, Chick 24
Davis, Alvin 82
Davis, Chili 85
Davis, George 4, 12
Davis, Glenn 84
Davis, Harry 2-5
Davis, Jody 82
Davis, Kiddo 31
Davis, Tommy 60-61
Dawson, Andre 75, 79, 85
Dayley, Ken 85
Dean, Dizzy (Jay) 30-35, 51
Dean, Paul 32
DeCinces, Doug 80, 84
Delahanty, Ed 43
Dempsey, Rick 81
Denny, John 74, 81
Dent, Bucky (Russell) 76
Derringer, Paul 29, 37-38, 43
Detroit Tigers (AL) 5-7, 9, 13-14, 21, 32-35, 38, 42-45, 48, 65-66, 70-71, 82, 85
Devlin, Art 3
DH (designated hitter) 71
Dickey, Bill 30, 35-36, 41, 52
Dietrich, Bill 35
DiHigo, Martin 75
Dillinger, Bob 45-47
DiMaggio, Dom 48
DiMaggio, Joe 34-40, 45-46, 48-50, 53
Dineen, Bill 1-3
Ditmar, Art 58
Doak, Bill 12, 19
Dobson, Chuck 69

Dobson, Pat 69
Doby, Larry 47, 50, 52
Dodgers—See Brooklyn Dodgers;
    Los Angeles Dodgers
Doerr, Bobby 41, 44, 84
Donlin, Mike 3
Donnelly, Blix 42
Donovan, Dick 59
Donovan, Wild Bill 5-6
Dorish, Harry 50
Dotson, Rich 81
Dougherty, Patsy 1, 6
Douglas, Phil 19
Downing, Al 62
Downing, Brian 80, 84
Doyle, Larry 9-10, 13
Drabowsky, Moe 64
Dropo, Walt 48
Drysdale, Don 57-58, 60-61, 63, 82
Duffy, Hugh 43
Duren, Ryne 56
Durham, Leon (Bull) 82
Durocher, Leo 52, 56
Dykes, Jimmy 27
Dykstra, Lenny 84

E

Earnshaw, George 27-29
Eason, Mal 4
Eastwick, Rawley 73-74
Eckersley, Dennis 86
Ehmke, Howard 21, 27
Eller, Hod 17
Elliott, Bob 45-46
Elliott, Claude 3
Ellis, Dock 68, 74
Ennis, Del 48
Epstein, Mike 70
Erskine, Carl 50-51, 54
Estrada, Chuck 58
Etten, Nick 41-43
Evans, Darrell 83-85
Evans, Dwight 84, 86
Evers, Johnny 5, 12, 44
Ewing, Buck 44

F

Faber, Red 15, 19-20, 62
Face, Roy 56, 58-60
Fain, Ferris 49-50
Fairly, Ron 63
Feller, Bob 36-39, 44-46, 49, 52, 60
Felsch, Happy 15, 17
Ferguson, George 4
Ferrell, Rick 82
Ferrell, Wes 29, 33
Ferriss, Boo 44
Fidrych, Mark 74
Figueroa, Ed 74-76
Fingers, Rollie 70-72, 75-76, 79-80
Fisher, Eddie 64
Fisk, Carleton 70, 73, 81
Fitzmorris, Al 74
Fitzsimmons, Freddie 31
Flanagan, Mike 77, 81
Flick, Elmer 2-4, 61
Flood, Curt 66
Fonseca, Lou 27
Ford, Dan 77
Ford, Whitey 48, 51, 53-56, 58-62, 66, 72
Fornieles, Mike 58
Forsch, Bob 76, 80-81
Forster, Terry 72, 76
Fosse, Ray 72
Foster, George 74-77
Foster, George (Rube) 13-14
Fournier, Jake 22
Fowler, Dick 43
Fox, Nellie 57
Fox, Pete 33
Foxx, Jimmy 27-33, 36-37, 49
Franco, John 86

Fraser, Chick 1
Freehan, Bill 66
Freeman, Buck 1-2
Freese, Gene 59
Frey, Lonny 38
Friend, Bob 53, 56, 58
Frisch, Frankie 19-21, 28-29, 32, 45
Frost, Dave 77
Fryman, Woodie 70
Furillo, Carl 45, 47, 51, 53

G

Gaetti, Gary 85
Galehouse, Denny 42
Galen, Augie 33, 35
Galvin, Pud 63
Garber, Gene 75, 80
Garcia, Mike 52
Gardner, Larry 14, 18
Garms, Debs 38
Garner, Phil 77
Garr, Ralph 72
Garvey, Steve 72, 75-76, 79, 82
Gedman, Rich 84
Gehrig, Lou 24, 26, 28-30, 32, 34-37, 39
Gehringer, Charlie 27, 32-33, 35, 47
Gelbert, Charley 28
Giants—See New York Giants;
    San Francisco Giants
Gibson, Bob 62, 65-66, 68, 79
Gibson, Kirk 82, 86
Gilliam, Junior 51
Giusti, Dave 69, 73
Gladden, Dan 85
Gladding, Fred 67
Gomez, Lefty 30-32, 35-36, 70
Gomez, Ruben 52
Gooden, Dwight (Doc) 82-83, 86
Goodman, Billy 48
Goodman, Ival 48
Gordon, Joe 35-36, 39-40, 46
Goslin, Goose 22-23, 26, 32-33, 66
Gossage, Goose 73, 76, 78-79, 82
Goudy, Hank 12
Granger, Wayne 68
Grant, Mudcat 63
Greenberg, Hank 32-33, 35-36, 38, 43-44, 54
Greenwell, Mike 86
Gregg, Vean 9
Grich, Bobby 77
Griffey, Ken 73-74, 78
Griffin, Alfredo 77
Griffith, Clark 44
Grim, Bob 52, 55
Grimes, Burleigh 18-19, 26, 29, 62
Grimsley, Ross 70, 72
Grissom, Marv 52
Groat, Dick 58
Groh, Heinie 17, 20
Gromek, Steve 46
Grove, Lefty 23-31, 33-34, 36-37, 45
Guerrero, Pedro 79, 81, 83
Guidry, Ron 75-79, 83
Guillen, Ozzie 83
Gullett, Don 71, 73-75
Gumbert, Harry 46
Gura, Larry 76, 78
Gwynn, Tony 82, 85-86

H

Haas, Mule 27-28
Hack, Stan 36-38, 43
Haddix, Harvey 57-58
Hadley, Bump 37
Hafey, Chick 26, 28-29, 69
Haid, Hal 30
Haines, Jesse 22, 24, 26, 29, 68
Halicki, Ed 73

Hall, Charley 8
Hall, Jimmie 63
Hallahan, Bill 28-29
Hamilton, Billy 59
Hamilton, Earl 10
Hammacker, Atlee 81
Hamner, Granny 48
Handley, Lee 37
Hansen, Ron 58
Hargrave, Bubbles 24
Hargrove, Mike 72
Harper, Tommy 67, 71
Harrelson, Ken 66
Harris, Bucky 22, 72
Harris, Joe 23
Harris, Mickey 44, 48
Hartnett, Gabby 33, 53
Hatten, Joe 45
Head, Ed 44
Hearn, Jim 48
Heath, Jeff 46
Heilmann, Harry 21, 23, 25, 50
Helms, Tommy 64
Henderson, Dave 84
Henderson, Rickey 78-84, 86
Hendrick, George 80
Hendrix, Claude 16
Henke, Tom 83, 85
Henley, Weldon 3
Henrich, Tommy 45, 47
Henry, Bill 59
Herman, Babe 30
Herman, Billy 33, 73
Hernandez, Keith 77, 80, 84
Hernandez, Willie 82
Herr, Tommy 83
Hershiser, Orel 83, 86
Herzog, Buck 10
Hess, Otto 4
Heusser, Ed 42
Higbe, Kirby 38-39
Higgins, Pinky 38
Higuera, Ted 86
Hill, Carmen 25
Hiller, Chuck 60
Hiller, John 71
Hisle, Larry 75
Hodges, Gil 47, 50-51, 53-55, 57
Hoerner, Joe 66
Hoffman, Danny 3
Hofman, Solly 8
Holland, Al 81
Hollocher, Charlie 16
Holloman, Bob 51
Holmes, Tommy 43
Holtzman, Ken 69-73
Honeycutt, Rick 81
Hooper, Harry 10, 13, 69
Hooton, Burt 70, 76, 79
Horlen, Joe 65
Horner, Bob 76, 80
Hornsby, Roger 17-24, 26-27, 40
Horton, Willie 66
Hough, Charlie 75
Houston Astros (NL) 60, 78-79, 84
Howard, Elston 60-61
Howard, Frank 58, 61, 66, 68
Howe, Steve 78-79, 81
Howell, Jay 86
Hoyt, LaMarr 80-81
Hoyt, Waite 20, 24-26, 67
Hrabosky, Al 73, 76
Hrbek, Kent 85
Hubbard, Cal 74
Hubbell, Carl 27, 31-32, 34-35, 45
Hubbs, Ken 60
Huggins, Miller 19, 62
Hughes, Jim 52
Hughes, Tom 1, 8, 13-14
Hughson, Tex 40, 44
Hunter, Catfish 69-74, 85
Hurst, Bruce 84, 86
Hurst, Don 30

I

Indians—See Cleveland Indians
Irvin, Monte 49, 71
Isbell, Frank 4

J

Jackson, Danny 83, 86
Jackson, Joe 17
Jackson, Larry 62
Jackson, Reggie 69-73, 75-76, 78, 80
Jackson, Travis 80
James, Bill 12
Jansen, Larry 49
Jay, Joey 59
Jenkins, Ferguson 65, 67, 69, 72
Jensen, Jackie 52-53, 56-57
Jethroe, Sam 48-49
John, Tommy 75-76, 78-79
Johnson, Alex 68
Johnson, Billy 41, 45
Johnson, Deron 63
Johnson, Judy 73
Johnson, Walter 8, 10-19, 21-23, 34
Johnstone, Jay 74
Jones, Cleon 67
Jones, Randy 73-74
Jones, Sad Sam 16, 20-21
Jones, Sam 53-54, 56-57
Jonnard, Claude 20-21
Jordan, Tim 4, 6
Joss, Addie 2, 5-6, 8, 76
Joyner, Wally 84

K

Kaat, Jim 63-64
Kaline, Al 53, 57, 66, 78
Kansas City Royals (AL) 53, 66, 74-76, 78, 82-83
Karl, Andy 43
Kauff, Benny 15
Keefe, Tim 62
Keegan, Bob 55
Keeler, Willie 3, 37
Kell, George 47, 81
Keller, Charlie 37, 39-41
Kelley, Joe 69
Kelly, George 19-22, 71
Kelly, King 43
Kelly, Pat 77
Keltner, Ken 46
Kennedy, Vern 33
Kerr, Dickie 18
Key, Jimmy 83, 85
Killebrew, Harmon 57, 60-62, 65, 67-69, 82
Killian, Ed 5
Kinder, Ellis 49, 51
Kiner, Ralph 44-50, 73
Kingman, Dave 77, 80
Kison, Bruce 77
Kittle, Ron 81
Klein, Chuck 27, 29-31, 77
Klieman, Ed 45
Kline, Ron 63
Klippstein, Johnny 58
Kluszewski, Ted 52, 57
Knight, Ray 84
Knott, Jack 33
Koenig, Mark 25
Konstanty, Jim 48
Koosman, Jerry 67, 71
Koslo, Dave 47
Koufax, Sandy 59-64, 70
Kramer, Jack 42
Krause, Harry 7
Kremer, Ray 23-25, 28
Krist, Howie 40
Kubek, Tony 55
Kucks, Johnny 54
Kuenn, Harvey 51, 57

Kuhel, Joe 31
Kurowski, Whitey 44
Kuzawa, Bob 50

L

Labine, Clem 51, 53-55
LaCoss, Mike 77
Lajoie, Nap 1-2, 35
Landis, Kennesaw Mountain 32
Langston, Mark 82, 84
Lanier, Max 41-42
Lansford, Carney 79
Larsen, Don 54-56
Lary, Frank 54
Lary, Lyn 34
Lavender, Jimmy 13
Law, Vernon 58
Lazzeri, Tony 24-25, 30, 34
Lea, Charlie 79
Lee, Bill (Big Bill) 33, 36
Lee, Bill (Spaceman) 73
Lee, Thornton 39
Leever, Sam 1
Lefebre, Jim 63
Lefferts, Craig 82
LeFlore, Ron 76, 78
Leibrandt, Charlie 83
Leifield, Lefty 7
Lemon, Bob 46, 48, 52-53, 74
Leonard, Buck 70
Leonard, Dennis 74-76, 78
Leonard, Dutch (Emil John) 33
Leonard, Dutch (Hubert Benjamin) 12, 14, 16
Leonard, Jeffrey 85
Lewis, Duffy 10, 13
Liddle, Don 52
Lindell, Johnny 45
Lindstrom, Ted 74
Lloyd, John Henry 74
Loes, Billy 50-51, 53
Lolich, Mickey 66, 69-70
Lollar, Sherm 57
Lombardozzi, Steve 85
Lonborg, Jim 65, 74
Lopat, Eddie 47-49, 51
Lopes, Davey 73-74, 76
Lopez, Al 75
Lopez, Hector 59
Los Angeles Angels (AL) 59, 68
Los Angeles Dodgers (NL) 56-57, 59-61, 63-64, 69, 72, 75-76, 78-79, 83, 86
Lown, Turk 57
Luderus, Fred 13
Lumley, Harry 2
Lundgren, Carl 1, 5
Luque, Dolf 21, 23
Lush, John 4
Luzinski, Greg 73, 75-76
Lyle, Sparky 70, 74-75
Lynn, Fred 73, 77, 80-81
Lyons, Ted 23-25, 40, 53

M

Mack, Connie 3, 8-9, 11, 27-28, 35
Maddox, Nick 5
Madlock, Bill 73-74, 77, 79, 81
Magee, Sherry 5, 8, 12, 16
Maglie, Sal 49, 52, 54
Magrane, Joe 86
Mails, Duster 18
Maisel, Fritz 12
Maldonado, Candy 85
Malone, Pat 27-28, 30, 34
Maloney, Jim 63
Maltzberger, Gordon 41
Mantle, Mickey 50-51, 53-56, 58-60, 62, 72
Manush, Heinie 24, 31, 62
Maranville, Rabbit 12, 52
Marberry, Firpo 22-24, 27, 30
Marichal, Juan 60-61, 66-67

Mariners—See Seattle Mariners
Marion, Marty 41-42
Maris, Roger 58-60, 62, 65
Marquard, Rube 9-11, 13, 69
Marshall, Mike 71-72, 77, 83, 86
Martin, Billy 51, 53, 75
Martin, Pepper 29, 31-32, 34
Mathewson, Christy 1-3, 5-11, 34
Matlack, Jon 70-71
Matthews, Eddie 51, 55, 57, 76
Matthews, Gary 71, 81
Mattingly, Don 82-83, 85
May, Jakey 22
May, Lee 68, 74
May, Rudy 78
Mayberry, John 74
Mayer, Erskine 13
Mays, Carl 13-14, 16, 18-19
Mays, Willie 49, 52-58, 60-64, 77
Mazeroski, Bill 58
Mazzilli, Lee 77
McBride, Bake 72, 78
McCahan, Bill 45
McCarthy, Joe 27, 30
McCarthy, Tommy 44
McCarver, Tim 62
McCaskill, Kirk 84
McCatty, Steve 79
McClain, Denny 66-67
McCormick, Frank 37-38
McCormick, Mike 58, 65
McCovey, Willie 57, 60-61, 66-67, 69, 84
McDaniel, Lindy 57-58, 61
McDonald, Jim 51
McDougald, Gil 49, 56
McDowell, Roger 84
McDowell, Sam 63-64, 66-68
McGann, Dan 3
McGee, Willie 80, 83, 85
McGinnity, Joe 1-5, 44
McGraw, John 2-3, 9, 11, 15, 19, 22, 35
McGraw, Tug 67, 71, 78
McGregor, Scott 77, 81
McGwire, Mark 85-86
McInnis, Stuffy 11-12
McKechnie, Bill 60
McLean, Larry 11
McMahon, Don 56-57
McManus, Marty 28
McNally, Dave 64, 67-69, 72
McNeeley, Early 22
McQuillen, George 8
McQuinn, George 42
McReynolds, Kevin 82, 86
Meadows, Lee 23, 25
Medwick, Joe 32, 34-36, 39, 66
Melton, Bill 69
Melton, Cliff 35
Merkle, Fred 9-10
Merritt, Jim 68
Mertes, Sam 1, 3
Mets—See New York Mets
Metzger, Butch 74
Meusel, Bob 19, 21, 23-26
Meusel, Irish (Emil) 19-22
Meyer, Jack 53
Meyer, Russ 51
Meyers, Chief 9, 11
Middleton, Jim 19
Milan, Clyde 10-11
Miller, Bing 27-28
Miller, Doc 9
Miller, Roscoe 1
Miller, Stu 56, 59-61, 64
Milwaukee Braves (NL) 51, 53-58, 68
Milwaukee Brewers (AL) 70, 79-80
Minnesota Twins (AL) 59-60, 62, 65, 67-68, 85-86
Minoso, Minnie 49-51, 55
Mize, Johnny 37-38, 40, 45-46, 48, 50, 79
Mizell, Vinegar Bend 58
Mogridge, George 16

Molitor, Paul 80
Monday, Rick 79
Montreal Expos (NL) 67, 79
Moon, Wally 52
Moore, Donnie 84
Moore, Earl 1, 8
Moore, Wilcy 25, 29-30
Moreno, Oscar 76-78
Moret, Roger 73
Morgan, Joe 70, 73-74, 81
Morris, Jack 81-82, 85
Morrison, Johnny 23, 27
Morton, Carl 68
Mostil, Johnny 23-24
Mueller, Don 42
Mullin, George 7, 10
Mungo, Van Lingle 34
Munson, Thurman 68, 74-75
Murphy, Dale 80-83
Murphy, Denny 8
Murphy, Johnny 36-37, 39-41
Murray, Eddie 75, 77, 79, 81
Murtaugh, Danny 39
Musial, Stan 40-42, 44, 46, 48-50, 53-55, 61, 67
Myer, Buddy 26, 33
Myers, Hi 17-18

N

Narleski, Ray 52-53
Neal, Charlie 57
Neale, Greasy 17
Nealon, Jim 4
Nehf, Art 19-20, 22
Nettles, Graig 74-76, 79
Newcombe, Don 47, 49, 53-54
Newhouser, Hal 42-44, 46
Newsom, Bobo 32, 38, 40
New York Giants (NL) 3-4, 6, 9-12, 14-16, 19-23, 26, 29, 31-32, 35, 48-50, 52, 56
New York Mets (NL) 60, 67, 71, 84, 86
New York Yankees (AL) 2, 4, 8, 19-22, 24-27, 29-32, 34-41, 45, 47-62, 74-76, 78-79
Nichols, Chet 49
Nichols, Kid 47
Nicholson, Bill 41-43
Niedenfuhr, Tom 81
Niekro, Joe 77-78
Niekro, Phil 65, 67, 72, 75, 77, 80
Nokes, Matt 85
Nolan, Gary 68, 73-74
Norman, Fred 73
North, Billy 72, 74
North, Lou 19
Northrop, Jim 66
Nuxhall, Joe 42

O

Oakland Athletics (AL) 66, 69-73, 79, 86
O'Brien, Buck 10
O'Dell, Billy 56
Odom, Blue Moon 70
O'Doul, Lefty 27
Odwell, Fred 3
O'Farrell, Bob 24
Oglivie, Ben 78, 80
Ojeda, Bob 84
Oliva, Tony 62-63, 68-69
Oliver, Al 72, 80
Orioles—See Baltimore Orioles
Orosco, Jesse 84
O'Rourke, Jim 43
Orth, Al 4
Osteen, Claude 64
Otis, Amos 69, 74, 76, 78
O'Toole, Jim 59
Ott, Mel 30-36, 40, 49
Overall, Orval 5-7
Owen, Frank 4

P

Pafko, Andy 43
Page, Joe 45, 47
Paige, Satchel 69
Palmer, Jim 64, 67-69, 71, 73-75
Pappas, Milt 69-70
Parker, Dave 73, 75-77, 79, 83
Parnell, Mel 47
Pasqual, Camilo 59-61
Passeau, Claude 37, 43
Patek, Freddie 75
Patten, Casey 2
Pearson, Albie 56
Pearson, Monte 31, 34, 36-37
Peckinpaugh, Roger 23
Pena, Alejandro 82
Pena, Tony 85
Pendleton, Terry 85
Pennock, Herb 12, 21, 24-26, 30, 46
Pepitone, Joe 61-62
Perez, Tony 65, 68, 71, 73
Perranoski, Ron 61, 67-68
Perry, Gaylord 68-70, 76
Perry, Jim 58, 63, 67-68
Pesky, Johnny 44
Peters, Gary 61-62, 64
Pfeffer, Frank 5
Pfeffer, Jack 4-5
Philadelphia Athletics (AL) 1, 3, 5, 7-9, 11-12, 26-30, 53
Philadelphia Phillies (NL) 11, 13-15, 48, 74-76, 78-79, 81
Phillies—See Philadelphia Phillies
Phillippe, Deacon 1
Pierce, Billy 51, 53, 55, 60
Piniella, Lou 67
Pinson, Vada 59
Pipgras, George 25-26, 30
Pipp, Wally 14-15, 19-21
Pirates—See Pittsburgh Pirates
Pittsburgh Pirates (NL) 1, 3, 5-7, 10, 23, 25, 27, 30-31, 36, 56, 58, 68-69, 70, 72-73, 77, 86
Plank, Eddie 3, 9, 11-12, 44
Players' Strike 70, 79
Podres, Johnny 53, 55, 57, 61
Pollet, Howie 41, 44
Polo Grounds (N.Y., N.Y.) 32
Porterfield, Bob 51
Potter, Nels 42
Powell, Boog 64, 67-69
Powell, Ray 19
Pratt, Del 14
Puckett, Kirby 85
Puhl, Terry 78

Q

Quinn, Jack 29-30
Quisenberry, Dan 78, 80-83

R

Radatz, Dick 60, 62
Radbourn, Charlie 39
Raffensberger, Ken 11
Raines, Tim 79-82, 84-85
Raschi, Vic 46-51
Rawlings, Johnny 19
Reardon, Jeff 83, 85
Reds—See Cincinnati Reds
Red Sox—See Boston Red Sox
Reed, Ron 75-76, 81
Reese, Pee Wee 45, 47, 50, 82
Regan, Phil 64, 66
Rehm, Flint 24
Reiser, Pete 39-40, 44
Reniff, Hal 61
Reulbach, Ed 4-6
Reuss, Jerry 73, 79
Reynolds, Allie 41, 45, 47-51
Reynolds, Carl 36

Reynolds, Harold 85
Rhoden, Rick 75
Rhodes, Bob 6
Rhodes, Dusty 52
Rice, Jim 73, 75-76, 81, 84
Rice, Sam 18, 23, 61
Richard, J. R. 76-77
Richardson, Bobby 58-60, 62
Riddle, Elmer 39
Righetti, Dave 79, 84
Ripken Jr., Cal 80-81
Rivera, Jim 53
Rivers, Mickey 73, 75
Rixey, Eppa 20, 61
Rizzuto, Phil 40, 48-49
Roberts, Robin 48, 50-53, 74
Robertson, Bob 68-69
Robertson, Charlie 20
Robertson, Dave 15
Robinson, Brooks 62, 64, 67-69, 81
Robinson, Frank 54, 59, 64, 67-69, 80
Robinson, Jackie 43, 45, 47, 50, 53, 60
Robinson, Wilbert 43
Roe, Preacher 43, 47, 50-51
Roenicke, Gary 81
Rogers, Steve 79-80
Rogovin, Saul 49
Rojas, Minnie 65
Rolfe, Red 34
Rommel, Ed 20, 23, 27
Root, Charlie 25, 27, 30
Rose, Pete 61, 66-67, 70-71, 73-74, 78, 83
Rosen, Al 48, 50-52
Roth, Braggo 13
Roush, Edd 15, 17, 60
Rowe, Schoolboy 32-33, 38
Royals—See Kansas City Royals
Rucker, Nap 6
Rudi, Joe 72
Rudolph, Dick 12
Ruether, Dutch 17, 23
Ruffing, Red 30, 34-38, 40, 65
Runnels, Pete 58, 60
Rusie, Amos 75
Russell, Allan 17, 21
Russell, Bill 72, 76
Russell, Jack 31
Russo, Marius 31
Ruth, Babe 13-14, 16-22, 24-32, 34, 37, 59
Ruthven, Dick 76, 78
Ryan, Nolan 70-77, 79, 85-86
Ryan, Rosy 20-21

S

Saberhagen, Bret 83
Sabo, Chris 86
Sadecki, Ray 62
Sain, Johnny 45-46, 51-52
Sallee, Slim 10, 12, 15, 17
Sandberg, Ryne 82
Sanders, Ken 69
Sanders, Ray 42
Sanford, Jack 55, 60
San Francisco Giants (NL) 56, 60, 63-66, 69, 85
Sanguillen, Manny 68-69
Santiago, Benito 85
Sauer, Hank 50
Sax, Steve 80
Schalk, Ray 53
Schantz, Bobby 50, 55, 58
Scheckard, Jimmy 1
Schmidt, Mike 72-75, 78-79, 81-82, 84
Schmitz, Johnny 44
Schoendienst, Red 43, 48, 56
Schulte, Fred 31

Schulte, Wildfire 8-9
Schumacher, Hal 31, 35
Schupp, Ferdy 15
Schwall, Don 59
Scioscia, Mike 86
Score, Herb 53-54
Scott, George 73
Scott, Jack 20-21
Scott, Jim 12
Scott, Mike 84
Seaton, Tom 11
Seattle Mariners (AL) 67-68
Seaver, Tom 65-69, 71, 73-74, 76-77, 79
Segui, Diego 68
Senators—See Washington Senators
Sewell, Joe 75
Seymour, Cy 3
Shannon, Mike 65
Shaw, Bob 57
Shawkey, Bob 12, 14, 18, 20
Shea, Specs 45
Sherdel, Bill 18, 24-26
Sherry, Larry 57
Shocker, Urban 18-20, 24-25
Shore, Ernie 13-15
Shoun, Clyde 37, 42
Show, Eric 82
Siebert, Sonny 64
Sievers, Roy 47, 55
Simmons, Al 27-29, 32, 51
Simmons, Curt 48, 62
Simpson, Wayne 68
Singer, Bill 68
Singleton, Ken 77
Sisler, George 16, 18-21, 25, 37
Sizemore, Ted 67
Skinner, Bob 58
Skowron, Moose 54-56, 58
Slagle, Jimmy 5
Slaughter, Enos 40, 44, 51, 83
Smith, Dave 84
Smith, Elmer 18
Smith, Frank 3, 6-7
Smith, Lee 81-82
Smith, Ozzie 83
Smith, Reggie 75
Snider, Duke 47-48, 50-51, 53-54, 57, 78
Southworth, Billy 24
Spahn, Warren 45-51, 55-56, 58-59, 71
Spalding, Albert 39
Speaker, Tris 10, 13-15, 18, 21, 35
Splitorff, Paul 75-76
St. Louis Browns (AL) 20, 25, 42
St. Louis Cardinals (NL) 24, 26, 28-29, 32-33, 37, 40-47, 61-62, 65-66, 80, 83, 85
Stafford, Bill 60
Stahl, Jake 8, 10
Staley, Gerry 57
Stallard, Tracy 59
Stanhouse, Don 77
Stargell, Willie 68-73, 77, 86
Staub, Rusty 71
Steinbach, Terry 86
Steinfeldt, harry 4
Stengel, Casey 21, 47, 56, 60, 72
Stephens, Vern 42-43, 47-48
Stephenson, Riggs 30
Stewart, Dave 81, 85-86
Stieb, Dave 83
Stirnweiss, Snuffy 42-43
Stone, George 4
Stone, Steve 78
Strawberry, Darryl 81, 84, 86
Stuart, Dave 58
Stuart, Dick 61
Sturdivant, Tom 54-55
Sullivan, Frank 53

Summers, Ed 6-7
Sundberg, Jim 83
Sutcliffe, Rick 77, 80, 82, 85
Sutter, Bruce 77-80, 82
Sutton, Don 72, 75-76, 78
Swan, Craig 76
Swoboda, Ron 67

T

Tanana, Frank 73, 75, 85
Tannehill, Jesse 2
Taveras, Frank 75
Tekulve, Kent 77
Tenace, Gene 70, 73
Terrell, Walt 85
Terry, Bill 28-29, 31, 39, 52
Terry, Ralph 59-60
Tesreau, Jeff 10-11
Texas Rangers (AL) 70
Thevenow, Tommy 24
Thomas, Gorman 77, 80
Thompson, Hank 52
Thompson, Sam 72
Thomson, Bobby 49
Tiant, Luis 66, 70, 73
Tidrow, Dick 74
Tigers—See Detroit Tigers
Tinker, Joe 6, 44
Tinkers-to-Evers-to-Chance 5, 8
Tobin, Jim 42
Toronto Blue Jays (AL) 83
Torre, Joe 69
Torrez, Mike 75
Trammell, Alan 82, 85
Traynor, Pie 22-23, 25, 46
Tresh, Tom 60, 62
Trillo, Manny 78
Trosky, Hal 34
Trout, Dizzy 41-43
Trucks, Virgil 43, 47, 50
Tudor, John 83
Tuero, Oscar 17
Turley, Bob 52-53, 56, 58
Turner, Jim 35, 43
Twins—See Minnesota Twins
Tyler, Lefty 16

U

Uhle, George 21, 24

V

Valenzuela, Fernando 79, 82-84
Vance, Dazzy (Clarence Arthur) 20-26, 28, 53
Vander Meer, Johnny 36, 39-41
Vaughan, Arky (Joseph Floyd) 33, 39, 41, 83
Vaughn, Jim (Hippo) 15-17
Veach, Bobby 13, 15-17
Veale, Bobby 62
Verban, Emil 42
Vernon, Mickey 33, 51
Versalles, Zoilo 63
Viola, Frank 85-86
Virdon, Bill 42
Voiselle, Bill 42
Vosmik, Joe 33
Vuckovich, Pete 80

W

Waddell, Rube 1-5, 44
Wagner, Honus 1-2, 4-7, 9, 34
Walberg, Rube 27, 29
Walker, Bill 27, 29
Walker, Dixie 42, 45
Walker, Harry 44-45

Walker, Tilly 16
Wallace, Bobby 51
Walsh, Ed 4-6, 8-10, 44
Walters, Bucky 37-38, 42
Waner, Lloyd 25, 65
Waner, Paul 25, 32, 34, 50
Ward, Aaron 21
Ward, Monte 62
Warneke, Lon 30, 33, 39
Washington Senators (AL) 10-11, 22-23, 28, 31, 41, 43, 59, 70
Watkins, George 28
Watson, Bob 79
Weiss, Walt 86
Welch, Bob 76, 83, 86
Welch, Mickey 71
Werber, Billy 32-33, 35, 38
Wertz, Vic 52
Wheat, Zack 14, 16, 18, 57
Whitaker, Lou 76, 84
White, Bill 62
White, Doc 4-5
White, Frank 83
Whitehill, Earl 31
White Sox—See Chicago White Sox
Wilcox, Milt 82
Wilhelm, Hoyt 50, 52, 56-57, 83
Wilks, Ted 42, 49
Willett, Ed 7
Williams, Billy 59, 70, 85
Williams, Cy 18, 21, 25
Williams, Earl 69
Williams, Ken 20
Williams, Lefty 17
Williams, Ted 37, 39-40, 44-48, 54-56, 64
Willis, Vic 7
Wills, Maury 58-64
Wilson, Don 65
Wilson, Earl 65
Wilson, Hack 24-28, 77
Wilson, Jim 52
Wilson, Willie 77-78, 80, 83
Wiltse, George 6
Winfield, Dave 77, 79
Wise, Rick 73
Witt, Mike 84
Wood, Smoky Joe 9-10, 13
Wood, Wilbur 70-71
Woodeshick, Hal 62
Woodling, Gene 47-48, 50
Worrell, Todd 83-85
Worthington, Al 63, 66
Wright, George 35
Wright, Glenn 23, 25
Wyatt, John 65
Wyatt, Whitlow 39
Wynn, Early 48, 52, 55-57, 70
Wynn, Jimmy 72
Wyse, Hank 43

Y

Yankees—See New York Yankees
Yankee Stadium (N.Y., N.Y.) 21
Yastrzemski, Carl 61, 65-66, 68, 73, 86
York, Rudy 38, 40-41, 43-44
Young, Cy 1-2, 6, 35
Youngs, Ross 19, 70
Yount, Robin 80

Z

Zachary, Tom 22, 26
Zachry, Pat 74
Zahn, Geoff 80
Zernial, Gus 49
Zimmerman, Heinie 10, 14-15
Zisk, Richie 72
Zuverink, George 54

DATE DUE

FE 15 '91		
MR 28 '91		
MY 3 '91		
DE 18 '92		
FE 24 '95		
OC 25 '96		
MY 23 '97		
MR 13 '98		
MY 05 '99		